GOING
CLASSIC

GOING
CLASSIC

The Essential Guide to Buying, Owning and Enjoying a Classic Car

Alan Anderson

Front cover images left to right:
Ford Escorts (MagicCarPics); Jaguar E-Type (Fiennes Restoration Ltd, fiennes.co.uk); Ford Zephyr (author's own)
Back cover images left to right:
MGB GT (author's own); Caterham 7 (Caterham Cars); a classic car show (author's own)

First published 2021

The History Press
97 St George's Place, Cheltenham,
Gloucestershire, GL50 3QB
www.thehistorypress.co.uk

British Library Cataloguing in Publication Data.
A catalogue record for this book is available from the British Library.

ISBN 978 0 7509 9680 8

Typesetting and origination by The History Press
Printed in Turkey by Imak.

CONTENTS

FOREWORD

Owning classic car is one of the most pleasurable and exciting means of motoring today – so long as you do it right. This book, *Going Classic*, written by Alan Anderson, a leading classic car journalist, covers just about all an enthusiast – novice or experienced – needs to know, written in an easy to follow and digest style.

After being approached by Air TV, *Bangers & Cash* was created to follow our family business and the day-to-day enquiries of buying and selling classic vehicles. Our auction sees every kind of motor – from an outlandish Excalibur Roadster that once belonged to Roy Orbison, to collections of British classics that have lurked undisturbed in garages for years. Some vehicles have certainly seen better days, but they all have their own value, and to the classic car community, they're a hidden treasure.

This guide is a useful tool to any prospective and current classic car owner, with advice and suggestions. If you're considering buying a classic vehicle, take a look at the Hot 100 list, there's one for everyone.

Derek Mathewson
Bangers & Cash
June 2021

www.mathewsons.co.uk

INTRODUCTION

Yearn to own a classic car? You're not alone. It's reported that there are around 1.5 million historic vehicles in Britain and, despite the recent global upheaval, the classic car scene is in better shape than ever. Rather than being simply another elitist hobby, it accounts for a whopping £7.2 billion contribution to the UK economy, supporting nearly 35,000 jobs and some 4,000 businesses in 2019. It is pretty serious fun in other words.

Going Classic is for the first-timer who wants to own a classic but needs help and questions answered before taking the plunge. Everything that you need to know is contained within these pages in an informative yet easy reading style: which classic suits you the best, choosing the perfect make and model, where to buy and why, how to buy a good one, how to strike the best finance deal, what equipment to carry about with you, making your classic earn its keep, classic insurance explained, plus even how to compete in classic motorsport – and much more!

Rounding off *Going Classic* is the 'Hot 100' hit list, which is a diverse selection of the top classics to buy and why. There is a classic with your name on it in there.

Whether it's a frumpy 1950s family saloon or a sexy, stylish '60s sports car, there is a classic that is just right for you.

A classic commercial will get you noticed and promote your business or trade at the same time.

PART 1

WHY GO CLASSIC?

Ask anyone who owns a classic car and penny to a pound they are likely to say that the experience enriches their lives and they are loath to be without one as a result. In these fast-changing times, where motoring is becoming something antisocial and to be endured rather than enjoyed, there's nothing like owning a classic car to bring back the joy of driving. It doesn't matter whether it's a Ford or a Ferrari, a Reliant or a Rolls, everybody's welcome to this hobby which evokes such fond memories and friendship.

A classic is the perfect antidote to hectic modern motoring, and life in the slow lane is as relaxing as it is enjoyable because, in many respects, you have to learn to drive all over again to master an old car.

Life in the slow lane is the antidote for today's fast-paced and highly charged roads. Modern motoring can be such a hectic, humourless affair, not helped by similar computer-styled 'repmobiles', which are high on efficiency but low on individual style and character. And while the driving dynamics of such cars are not in question, they demand increasingly little driver input. Happily, a classic is the complete opposite, demanding your attention, adaptation and enthusiasm, because every oldie will develop their own foible or idiosyncrasy that becomes part of their charm whenever you're out on a drive. You know that you've *driven* a classic after any journey and that is where the real pleasure lies.

Clockwise from above: Acting the part is all part of the fun and many events actively encourage dressing in period; If you don't fancy getting your hands dirty, a good number of small, local garages can easily cater for classics and at extremely keen prices; Shows are major part of the classic car scene and hugely enjoyable, especially if you are a member of a classic car club and are invited to display your pride and joy on a stand.

Yet classic motoring extends far further than driving. In an age where even experienced motorists are fearful of opening the bonnet if a fault crops up, almost any half-competent enthusiast can work on a classic – and gain a lot pleasure and satisfaction from doing so. Furthermore, you can actually work and fix that piece of Meccano-like machinery armed with just the simplest of tools, much more satisfying than simply staring at the plastic-hooded technophobia-inducing power unit of today that's crowded by relays, wiring and computer plug-in points.

A classic appeals as much to the head as to the heart. While it's wrong to say that all collectibles are a licence to print money, history shows that many owners have seen their hobby become financially attractive, making a tidy profit where Capital Gains Tax does not apply – or at worst, cost them nothing. A classic may even become something to keep forever and become a profitable heirloom in the process.

Whether it's a Morris Marina or a McLaren, the camaraderie between classic petrolheads is deep rooted, never more so than if you join one of the hundreds of car clubs. Marque-specific ones mean you can benefit in so many ways, including technical help, parts supply, invitations to car shows and much more. Indeed, countless members have struck up lifelong friendships as a result of owning a classic, and for many the social scene becomes a key reason for having one. Isn't it time that you discovered what you've been missing for so long?

WHAT CLASSIC?

Buying and owning a classic car is a very personal and emotive pastime and every enthusiast has a personal favourite car or commercial vehicle. Selecting the right one in a cold, clinical way doesn't really apply as it does with a modern daily driver. If you yearn for a Jaguar E-Type or MGB then there's going to be little to dissuade you! That said, unless your heart is totally set on a particular make and model, then it is best to compile a shortlist of candidates that may also satisfy you if you can't find the right 'number one' choice.

By and large, the majority of enthusiasts hanker for one particular make of sports car or sports saloon that they have dreamed about, perhaps since childhood. Others like to chop and change every so often to savour the sheer variety of classics on offer, or perhaps build up a small fleet to satisfy their moods. If the latter is part of your game plan, then why not? So long as you have enough storage space that is. Those who have gone down that route normally advise on keeping the fleet small, perhaps no more than four vehicles, as you can only drive one at a time and it is easy to forget and neglect your less favourite classic(s).

Traditional or modern? Classics can bring out the ageist in us as we all have our own individual views on how old a car has to be before it can be regarded as one. The general view, given

Clockwise from top: By and large, British classics are the best to own because spare parts are more plentiful and easier to obtain; If you want the most metal for your money, a modern classic from the new millennium, like this Jaguar S-Type, have much to offer and, if you look after it, will ultimately appreciate in value and possibly require no major restoration either; Modern classics, such as this early 1980s Vauxhall Astra GTE, are becoming increasingly popular, liked for their more modern manners and safety features.

by classic car insurers at least, is 25 years, but there is no hard and fast rule here. What isn't in dispute is the sharp rise in popularity of modern classics or 'Youngtimers' amongst those under 30 years old, who regard established icons like MGBs and Capris as relics and want the performance, refinement and safety offered by vehicles made from the 1980s onwards. Another benefit is the usually tempting prices, particularly on models which haven't yet reached classic status and so are valued low, perhaps not much more than 'banger' money. Play your cards right and by purchasing well and looking after it, a modern classic may never require a costly full restoration, thus preserving its originality – which will count for a lot in years to come. The flip side is that the car may not qualify for classic insurance and parts availability probably won't be as good as a traditional collectible.

A modern classic is the more suitable choice for those intending to use one as a daily driver, although many enthusiasts happily run oldies from the 1960s and '70s, thus benefitting from road fund licence and MOT exemption. While potentially saving hundreds of pounds each year sounds tempting, the financial advantages are outweighed by the fact that the car is in use far more and will incur more frequent servicing and repair costs as a consequence.

There is also an emotive issue to contend with. It's a personal thing, but the majority of classic enthusiasts like to save their collectibles for special occasions such as a Sunday treat. Familiarity breeds contempt goes the old saying, and this certainly goes for cars. By using your classic as a mere daily driver you are in grave danger of subconsciously viewing it as any old hack, and as it wears out (as it inevitably will), you'll be considering selling it – just like the previous owners did!

CHECKING OVER A CLASSIC CAR

No matter how exclusive (or expensive) that classic you have hunted down and desperately want to have as your own, it's still another second-hand car at the end of the day and it needs to be viewed and regarded as such. Rein in your emotions and look at the vehicle in a cool, calm and collected way as you would (and should) your next daily driver. Unless it's truly exceptional, or you know the vehicle in question, don't buy the first one you see. Instead, check out a few examples to set a reliable benchmark, as they will vary greatly. Better still, why not consider hiring your chosen classic(s) from one of the numerous classic hire fleets (see separate chapter on page 31), if only for a day, to see if one of the selected vehicles really is your dream drive after all?

While the excitement is hard to contain, you need to treat the purchase of a dream classic as you would any second-hand vehicle.

A pile of receipts is a sure sign of a caring owner(s), as it is clear evidence of any major repairs to the bodywork and chassis.

A crafty way to ascertain the quality of a classic is to inspect often-overlooked details, such as the finish of the petrol filler area. This Aston is as good as the rest of the car!

Ownership and authenticity come first. Is the current owner or seller registered on the V5c (log book), and are they legally entitled to sell the vehicle – is finance still owing on it, for example? If you are in any doubt, have a data check from the likes of HPI or AA/RAC carried out to verify the classic's 'honesty'. It will highlight previous crash damage, outstanding finance and whether it's been stolen in its life (theft for complete vehicles or for their parts is soaring). The check will be at your expense, of course, but it could save thousands in the long run in terms of money and worry.

Is the vehicle what it purports to be? Desirable mainstream classics, typified by the Mini Cooper S, Lotus Cortina and later RS Fords, are easily cloned and passed off as the real thing – some so convincingly that even the experts can't spot the difference. Check that the chassis numbers tally and have an owners' club expert verify the car's authenticity (they'd know all the intricate detail changes) if in the slightest doubt. If the seller is uncooperative then it is best to walk away and find another.

First impressions count. Does the classic (car, van or even lorry for that matter) send out the right signals, and is it as advertised? Does it look genuine or is it simply tarted up for sale? Is the vendor someone you wish to have dealings with? There's an old adage that nice people sell nice things and it's as true today as it ever was. Depending on the classic and its age, the number of owners and mileage are secondary to its provenance and service history. If the vehicle has been restored, a good owner will have kept a portfolio of pictures as proof, along with any relevant invoices pertaining to parts bought and previous work carried out.

Little things can sometimes tell a lot. For instance, are the tyres not only in good condition and less than 8 years old (the date should be found on the tyre's sidewall) but are they also of a known make, ideally of the same manufacturer all round or at least on the same axle? Odd tyres can really make a vehicle handle poorly, plus it points to a less than caring ownership.

Nine times out of ten, the bodywork is the most worrisome point. Mechanical parts can invariably be replaced or repaired, but bodywork issues can send any classic to the crusher. The trick is to separate the critical from the cosmetic. Start by finding out the relevant weak spots of your chosen vehicle as well as the obtainability of replacement panels. Again, an owners' club can provide invaluable help here.

Rust is the main worry with any classic – you have to segregate the structural from the cosmetic. The biggest fear should be poor repairs as they give a false impression and will have to be carried out again properly.

By and large, the most crucial areas relate to the vehicle's structure, including the chassis, inner panels (wings and sills), box sections, suspension and steering attachment points, floorpans, cross-members and bulkheads. It is highly likely that past repairs have been carried out, so check the quality of the work. Look for recent repairs, perhaps simply to obtain an MOT certificate, and be very suspicious of fresh, thick underseal that may be masking bad rot or poor-quality repairs.

Mainly cosmetic rather than serious, although still difficult and dear to rectify, is rust in non-structural areas like wheel arches, wings, sills (outer), boot, bonnet, doors and suchlike. Filler work is common here so a crafty tool to keep about your person is a small magnet to check for filler. Has a recent respray (complete or part) been carried out to gloss over the poor state of the body-work? Even if the classic is sound and smart, don't dismiss cruddy chrome work as it can cost as

Above: A frequently missed point is the state of the boot compartment and the condition of the jack and tools. This Vauxhall Viva is spot on, plus it has the correct rubber matting – many are carpeted instead because it's easier.

Opposite: Don't ignore the interior as it is where you will spend most of your time and can be as costly to refurbish as the exterior. This Jaguar XK is better than new although many enthusiasts prefer an original patina as well as a 'lived-in' look instead.

While classics more than 40 years old do not legally require an annual MOT, good owners still keep up this practice and it is a point in their favour. If the owner is agreeable, have one carried out before purchase at your expense.

much as body repairs to replace or rectify. Similarly, don't overlook an aged interior for the same reasons, as even what may seem like a mere detail, such as broken dials or switchgear, can prove surprisingly expensive and irksome to put right. Play around with all the switches for features like wipers, electric windows and air conditioning to see that they all work how they should. Good signs include a tidy boot or luggage area with all tools present and correct, and a clean, but not over-glossy, engine compartment with all the fluids clean and up to their proper levels.

Checking out an old classic isn't quite the same as your next daily driver, so if you feel you are out of your depth, have a classic garage or specialist do it for you rather than a normal AA/RAC inspection service, which will quite possibly be of minimal use on very old classics. If you desire more assurance, why not ask the vender to have the vehicle MOT tested, even if it's exempt from the check? It'll be at your expense, but for around £50 it's money well spent, and if the seller isn't okay with the idea then you should draw your own conclusions ...

THE TEST DRIVE

This is the part buyers are itching to get on with – but don't be! Take your time and do it methodically. Begin with starting the engine from stone cold to check for undue noises and how long it takes the oil warning light (has it been disconnected?) along with any other driver lights, such engine management, ABS and so on, to extinguish.

Don't be too eager to jump into the hot seat. For a start, unless you are buying from a trader, you may not be insured to drive a vehicle not belonging to you (check your own cover beforehand), and check other legalities such as current MOT and road tax if applicable. Also bear in mind that unless you are experienced in driving 'oldies', it will feel very strange, plus you may be driving on new roads. So let the owner/trader take the first stint while you concentrate on how the car is performing.

A test drive is a must, but do ensure you are insured beforehand. Make suitable allowances for the vehicle's age, but also make sure it performs like it should. Finally, do you actually like it? If not, don't buy and have a rethink on what classic floats your boat.

Now it's your turn! Are you comfortable – that's very important – and is there enough fuel for a good twenty-minute drive on varying roads? A quick gallop around the block isn't sufficient and if the vendor doesn't agree to this, perhaps find another car and seller.

OUR TOP TEST-DRIVING TIPS

◎ Does the vehicle feel right and perform like it ought to? Again, driving a few to set a benchmark is wise. Is the oil pressure healthy, and does the warning light extinguish quickly on start-up and not illuminate at low speeds when up to temperature?

◎ Keep a watchful eye on the temperature gauge as classics can be prone to overheating. If okay, it should sit around midway and not rise unduly under fast driving. On the other hand, if the needle refuses to leave the cold sector, it may be that the thermostat has been removed to keep the engine artificially cool.

◎ On the move, can you hear a rumbling sound? This may suggest a worn crankshaft and bearings, signifying major engine wear. A lighter tapping sound originating from the top end of the engine is normally deterioration of tappets/camshaft and is usually less serious. On the move, when safe to do so, take your foot off the throttle and then 'floor it' while checking in the rear-view mirror for excessive smoking. If you have doubts about the engine's condition, have a compression test carried out if the vendor is agreeable.

◎ Certain noises and vibrations are a characteristic of many classics, especially transmissions. Is the gearchange quality okay? Do any gears jump out on the overrun (i.e. a closed throttle)? If automatic, does the transmission change gear smoothly without jerks or undue delay, and is the fluid clean or does it smell sour or burnt?

◎ It depends on the vehicle in question, but overall is it responsive and precise without undue slack, with no detectable wandering or crabbing (maybe suggesting a wonky or badly repaired chassis)? Does the car pull to one side, which can be due to anything from simply poor steering alignment to a broken or buckled chassis, and is the power steering (if fitted) smooth and consistent?

◎ Brakes must pull up the vehicle squarely and progressively, suggesting a well-serviced and adjusted system. Juddering usually points to worn drums or discs but can be due to a long lay-up. If possible, remove the wheels to check visually. The fluid should be clean and up to the mark.

- See that the vehicle sits at an even stance without listing or sagging (usually at the rear), which suggests worn or broken suspension springs. Have new parts been fitted? If it appears the majority of one side of the suspension has been replaced, it could be due to past damage against a high kerb. Press down firmly on each corner to check if the body moves up and down; it should do so no more than twice. When on a test drive, is the suspension working as it should with no undue clonks, creaks, crashes and so on?

- Once the test drive is completed, park up and let the engine idle, watching for a low oil pressure, a rising coolant temperature and any flickering warning lights. With the bonnet up, look for fluid leaks and remove the oil filler cap to check for undue smoking and fuming. Switch off and restart the engine; it should fire up instantly. If it struggles, it points to a fuel-system fault such as a worn carburettor or ill-tuned fuel injection.

- Always bear in mind that even concours classics will have some faults, so don't expect perfection, especially on older vehicles. Finally, even if the vehicle of your dreams checks out okay, did you actually like driving it? That's vital! If you are having second thoughts, walk away now and have a rethink on your choice of classic as you'll only become disillusioned and sell it on, maybe at a loss.

HOW TO FINANCE WITHOUT FEAR

There are two types of classic car buyer: those that can afford one with cash at the ready, and those that can't. Most, like me, sadly fall into the latter category, but the good news is that raising the readies has never been easier or cheaper.

Low-cost loans are everywhere and by studying the market you can save a bundle on interest changes, plus, due to their appreciating nature, some special finance contracts are applicable to classics. Your credit worthiness plays a big role. If you have a sufficient credit limit, a zero per cent loan, the type that are widely offered by credit-card companies – including supermarkets – may

The beauty of a classic is that usually any finance charges can be counteracted by rising car values, so in effect you may enjoy a 'free' hobby.

A good specialist or dealer will offer a finance package, although you'd be better to shop around as it's an ever-competitive market. Remember, it's the APR that counts the most when comparing deals.

make the most sense of all, providing you can pay the debt off during the stipulated time as you'll incur high charges otherwise.

A bank loan is the most straightforward finance method although it's possible to obtain personal loans from other sources, such as credit card and finance houses. Usually, a personal loan will be 'unsecured', meaning you will not have to put up a guarantee or any security, such as your house. Hire Purchase (HP) means that the vehicle being financed is used as security for the loan and will appear on the HPI register. Obviously, the longer the period of the loan, the more interest you will pay over the period.

A Balanced Payments Finance lease is similar to HP, but interest is calculated on a daily basis on the ever-reducing balance. However, the interest rate is variable throughout the contract, so, unlike a conventional HP agreement, if interest rates rise sharply (unlikely in the current climate), then either the repayments will rise or the length of the agreement will be extended. Also, the minimum amount borrowed can be quite high. If you intend to keep the car more than three years, consider a straight HP loan.

What about extending your mortgage? Sometimes referred to as a second mortgage, this can seem logical for larger borrowing. As the name implies, the loan is usually secured on property, so this method of financing should only be used where there is a comfortable amount of equity available and the repayments are not going to be a problem over the term of the loan. On the other hand, if you fancy an expensive Aston Martin, it may be your only route to contentment as repayments can be set for as long as twenty-five years! Cashing in a pension also sounds tempting – and many have done so – but look longer term first before you do the same. Speak to a finance expert beforehand.

SIX OF THE BEST TIPS

- ◎ Make sure you can easily afford the loan, and choose a deal that strikes a realistic balance between a manageable monthly outgoing (don't forget other expenditures such as road tax, insurance, MOT and maybe storage) and the loan's total cost.
- ◎ Sort the money situation out before you go classic car hunting as it puts you in the driving seat for a better deal, plus it gives you time to shop around for the best package.
- ◎ Use cash if possible. It sounds old-fashioned but it's usually the cheapest policy in the long run and it's all 'done and dusted' then.
- ◎ Compare the total cost of the loan including interest rates, and not just the monthly payments.
- ◎ For comparisons, only use APRs to calculate interest being charged. Flat-rate calculations vary between lenders whereas APRs don't.
- ◎ Be aware that Personal Contract Plans (PCPs) will require you to pay a final lump sum (also known as a balloon payment) so make sure you can budget for it.

CLASSICS WORTH CONSIDERING

LEFT-HAND-DRIVE CLASSICS

Many think that having a left-hand-drive car in Britain is more trouble than it's worth, but in reality there are good reasons to buy an LHD classic. The obvious one is price, and with typical savings of up to almost a third, you could own a classic that you'd otherwise never be able to contemplate. With a good many Brits having holiday homes abroad, owning an LHD classic makes sound sense as the ideal car to use. Don't worry, it doesn't take long to get used to driving one in the UK – it's like driving a right-hand-drive car in Europe, albeit in reverse, and you soon adapt. There are downsides to consider as many insurers charge a premium (potentially up to a quarter) and you must declare that the car is LHD. Parts availability may pose a problem, making servicing slightly harder, but on the plus side LHD British classics command good prices outside the UK. If you're thinking of importing an LHD classic, especially from the US, there are pricey import duties and shipping costs to factor in.

Opposite: A left-hand-drive classic can be cheaper to buy although some service parts can prove harder to obtain. Converting to RHD is usually straightforward, although 'left hookers' find eager buyers on the Continent and are quite easy to adapt to on our roads.

PICKING A PROJECT

Many enthusiasts gain more satisfaction from restoring a classic to its former glory than owning and driving it, even though it takes years of sweat and tears. Don't automatically run away with the idea – as many do – that restoring your chosen classic is a sure-fire route to save money by saving on labour charges. While you can restore a classic on a budget, costs are bound to spiral so dial in some leeway. Think long term as well; it's better to spend £100 now than £400 later ...

In essence, there are three levels of restoration project: light, involved, and 'basket case' (a now archaic and little-used term, but the way they are still commonly referred to in the classic car scene). What determines your chosen path is your level of skill, your home garage facilities and the time you can allocate to the task.

Above left: If you fancy a challenge then a project to rebuild and restore brings as much satisfaction as driving a classic, but don't be under any misapprehension of the potentially mammoth task lying ahead. *Above right*: Although for the majority they are a summer treat, there's no reason you can't use a classic in any weather – even in deepest winter – so long as it's maintained well.

Light restoration work generally infers perhaps a bit of TLC all round along with some routine repairs to make good. Nothing too serious or costly is involved, and possibly the vehicle can still be used on the road while restoration and refurbishment is carried out. However, while many enthusiasts have successfully 'running restored' their classics, it's often far easier to lay the car up and do the job properly; the problem with rebuilding a road-legal classic is that you never know quite how far you can go without making it unusable. Remember, a half-hearted job is going to be a waste of time and money in the long run.

Involved means that there's serious work to be done. Adverts saying 'would suit an enthusiast' are the classic car equivalent of estate agent jargon and you shouldn't underestimate the task ahead, even if it's still a legal runner.

A *'basket case'* means that the vehicle is just that – a wreck that demands nothing less than a total rebuild, which will be costly and time-consuming. But then again, never look at classic car renovation as a short-term thing. Before you take the plunge, sit down and think carefully about the project and what you can or can't do – and form some sort of plan to see it through.

One possible solution is to opt for what's called a 'part restoration'. This is where a previous owner has purchased a project with all the best intentions, but for whatever reason couldn't see the job though – but not after spending a lot of time and money on parts and repairs. Usually a part restoration is sold at a loss so a canny enthusiast can pick up a bargain. Just don't let yourself fall into the same trap!

For the 'first timer' it's best to choose a popular classic such as an MG, Triumph, Morris Minor, etc., which is simply constructed and requires the minimum of special tools, for which spare parts are plentiful and reasonably priced, and which is backed by a good specialist and owners' club scene. Most importantly, never lose sight of the fact that this is supposed to be an enjoyable hobby, intended to ease the tensions of modern life – not create more! But whatever project route you choose, ensure that even if it comes as a box of bits, the right documents and proof of ownership come with the ignition keys. As for deciding a project's real-world worth, speak to a specialist or owners' club to get a guide as it's easy to pay too much for a non-runner.

Finally, let's end with a gentle word of advice: do not procrastinate! While you should never rush the job or make it an act of duty, it's a fact proven time and time again that if you haven't made decent headway with any project within the first three months or so, then it's odds on that you'll never see it through to the bitter end ... as many have sadly discovered.

RIGHTING A WRITE-OFF

If you intend to restore a classic then why not consider rebuilding a write-off? Look at it this way: as restoring any oldie invariably entails making good the bodywork, what's the difference between renovating a rusty wreck and a crashed one? It's the same principle, albeit from a different perspective. You will have to watch what constitutes a write-off as the official DVLA alphabetical classifications will determine the vehicle's worth. The most severe are A and B, both meaning the vehicle isn't allowed back on the road ever again, and while other damage categories detailing lesser damage (C, N and S) are legally repairable, the V5c document will be duly stamped accordingly and perhaps devalue the vehicle, especially a modern classic.

Below L-R: A crashed classic can be a good buy, particularly if it's minor damage like this MGB's door. However, more serious injuries which affect the chassis are another matter, although it's really no different to restoring a badly rusted chassis, but approached from a different angle; A re-shell can save a lot of restoration hassle, but may affect the vehicle's originality and may well result in the loss of classic status; Fire damage can be much worse than it looks as it usually impacts the interior, wiring and engine compartment, perhaps melting the carburettors. If really severe, it can also buckle the chassis.

You can re-shell using either a second-hand or, if available, a brand-new body, but you can run into legality issues if the car is passed on as original. Worst of all, if it lacks the right documentation or parts invoices, all of which have to be submitted to the DVLA as proof, a re-shelled classic is in danger of losing its originality, which will invariably mean a Q registration number as opposed to a proper age-related plate. Usually reserved for kit cars, not only will a Q plate seriously devalue the vehicle, but it will also lose any exemption entitlements to road fund licence and MOT status. Also, you cannot substitute a 'Q plate' with a personalised registration number. However, the DVLA is happy to help and obtaining a copy of document INF 26 is the best starting point.

WHERE TO BUY A CLASSIC

Essentially, there are three ways to purchase a classic: private, auction and dealer, also known as the trade. All three options have their plus and minus points.

PRIVATE

Private sales remain the most popular method to purchase a classic although, unlike with a modern car, they don't automatically equate to cheaper prices when compared to a dealer. The main plus point is that – hopefully – you are able to meet the current owner and as a consequence gain a clearer, more comprehensive history of the vehicle. The seller's demeanour can give you a useful signal as to whether the vehicle (and seller) is honest or not. No warranties are given by a private sale, and you should be wary if one is implied as it will be meaningless in a court of law. Your only legal protection is whether the vehicle in question was described dishonestly in any advertisements under the Trades Description Act.

There's no shortage of classics being sold by their owners and shows are a popular place to unearth a good buy, but, unlike mainstream moderns, don't automatically expect lower prices compared to a dealer.

Above left: Auctions are an exciting place to buy but are fast moving, decisive and not for the ditherer, although they provide more safeguards than buying privately. Visit a few first as a 'dry run' to see if this method is for you.

Above right: A classic dealer is a big help for the first-time buyer, plus they can provide finance and part-exchange facilities. Warranties usually differ from the normal practice, but a good specialist will still look after you.

AUCTION

If you like the thrill of a high-speed sale and trying to outwit established traders, you'll love an auction. Certainly, it can net a good deal, but on the other hand, intense bidding can realise a price far higher that you'd bargained for, especially once auction fees and VAT are added to the final bill, a point overlooked by many. You have more consumer protection at an auction than buying privately because the vehicle must be described with accuracy, although no warranty will be given. Also, you need to have the necessary finance at hand and are required to remove the vehicle, either by driving or towing it away, at short notice. Bear in mind that, unlike conventional auctions, the vehicles remain static and are not started up or run so you need to have a good grasp of cars, a gut feeling and a bit of a lucky streak. The best way of achieving all three is to visit a few auctions as a 'dry run' to see if this fast-lane scene is right for you.

DEALERS

There's nothing more thrilling than visiting a car showroom to drool and dream. Good classic car dealers that you'll find in mainstream classic car magazines survive on their reputations and will have top-notch stock, or can obtain the classic of your dreams – given time. Generally, the cars for sale are ready to enjoy and will come fully prepped and refurbished with a fresh MOT. Finance and trade-in terms plus buy-back agreements are often provided as well, although not all traders provide written warranties, preferring a 'Gentlemen's agreement' instead. You'll have to decide if it's acceptable or not, but the majority of dealers are honourable folk and remember that you do have the full weight of consumer rights on your side if something goes wrong. Don't always assume that buying from a dealer is dearer than other purchasing avenues either, because the classic market can be a surprisingly level playing field when it comes to prices on the windscreen.

SELLING A CLASSIC

If anything, selling a classic is easier than a modern daily driver. A classic usually has a captive audience waiting and it's not unknown for owners to have prospective buyers queuing up when they decide to sell, especially if they are a member of an owners' club where word is spread about in forums and chat rooms. Another simple and easy way to offload a classic, assuming it's all clean and correct, is to exhibit at a classic show with a 'For Sale' sign clearly displayed. However, even this is too much hassle for some, who perhaps have had bad experiences of dealing with buyers or time-wasters in the past. The answer is to either have a classic dealer purchase it from you outright or sell it on your behalf.

The former is a simple trade-in, but the latter practice is known as Sale and Return, or sold 'by consignment or commission', and is very popular in classic car circles. Essentially, you entrust a trader to sell the vehicle on your behalf for a set price with any profit, or a fixed commission, going to the dealer – or return it if it isn't sold after a specified period. All the viewings and negotiations are handled by the trader, so no more waiting around for no-shows and tyre kickers. Not only that, you don't have to invite strangers into your home, either – a big plus for many these days. Furthermore, there's the likely probability that the specialist dealer can strike a better price than you can, so everybody wins.

There are downsides that you must consider, however. For starters, you have to hand over the vehicle with all the documents, etc., so it pays to ensure that the classic remains your property and not that of the trader. Keep a regular contract between you and the trader and make it crystal clear whose responsibility it is to insure the car – normally this will fall to the trader. On the other hand, if the car is entrusted to the dealer and it develops a fault that is not caused by them, the responsibility will lie with you to repair it, as it would if it were in your possession. Also dealers may insist on carrying out certain repairs or refurbishment to help achieve the best sale price, plus a service and perhaps an MOT, all at your expense, to protect the dealer's reputation.

Many traders operate consignment sales, if for no other reason than they simply don't have the capital to buy their expensive stock outright. One way to ascertain if a classic is being sold by consignment is whether POA (Price on Application) rather than a sticker price is displayed on the advert. There's nothing wrong in consignment buying or selling, but you must choose a respected trader and have a binding contract drawn up, which states the agreed sale price, and insist that if the car is returned to you, unsold, no fee is incurred.

TOOLS AND WHAT TO CARRY IN YOUR CLASSIC

Anybody who wants to own a classic had better be prepared to learn to work on one. Even the least mechanically minded owner should be prepared to carry out some degree of roadside maintenance, even if it's something as simple as a tyre change. To enable this, you need to assemble a small toolkit that needn't prove extravagant or expensive.

First, find out whether your classic uses imperial or metric fixings so you can buy the correct spanners and socket set. As a rule, pre-1970s British classics will require 'AF' tools while later vehicles, along with European classics, require the metric equivalent.

A basic toolkit should comprise: a selection of open-ended spanners, various flat-blade and cross-head screwdrivers, a pair of combination pliers, a small hammer and a spark plug spanner. A small socket set will prove very useful and this can all be housed in a tool roll or small cantilever toolbox. Other useful items include insulating tape, a ball of string, cable ties, disposable gloves, a packet of wet wipes and perhaps a pair of disposable overalls to protect your clothes if you need to crawl underneath a vehicle for whatever reason.

From a safety angle, consider carrying a small bottle jack for wheel-changing purposes as the jacking points on older classics can be unsafe and give way due to hidden rust. A small first-aid kit, warning triangle, tow rope, torch, fuel can, water container (an old supermarket milk carton suffices) and roll of kitchen paper can also prove invaluable. Assemble an emergency spares kit of a fanbelt, bulbs and set of jump leads or, better still, a charged compact battery power pack. Don't worry, all this paraphernalia won't take up much space and will save a lot of time and hassle when out and about. Finally, always carry a well-charged mobile phone with you and consider having breakdown cover (although a classic insurance policy can provide this as part of the overall package).

Due to their simple make-up, the majority of classics are easy and, weather permitting, pleasurable to work on, requiring only basic tools and equipment.

WHY YOU NEED CLASSIC INSURANCE

One of the many plus points of owning a classic is the prospect of low-cost motoring in the shape of MOT and road-tax exemptions and inexpensive insurance cover. There's no shortage of specialist brokers (many offering advantageous terms via classic car owners' clubs) and insurers to keep premiums competitive. On the other hand, a typical classic car policy provides stricter cover and usage (e.g. annual mileage will be limited, storage stipulated and it probably will not cover you to drive other vehicles with third-party cover as conventional insurance does) than a mainstream type. Some classic insurance companies won't provide cover if you don't possess a daily driver or a company car – in other words, it may prove hard to obtain cover if the vehicle is intended to be your sole transport, and at which point cover prices may rise steeply.

However, one of the beauties of a classic car policy is that due to their specialist nature, plus the small percentage of claims made, the make and model is not as important as it is with a modern. For example, it may cost roughly the same to insure a powerful Triumph GT6 or TR6 as it would a slower Spitfire or Herald. What's more, many popular modifications, especially if they are for safety reasons (such as front disc brakes or improved suspension), won't result in a loaded premium either so always declare them.

Classic cars rise in value, which is why a classic insurer will want to agree a set value, potentially involving an independent inspection. More than likely, the company or broker will wish to see a collection of photographs to verify the vehicle's condition at the very least. Also, just because your dream classic is little more than a rolling wreck, or scattered about in assorted boxes in the garage, doesn't mean that it shouldn't be suitably insured. With barn-find Aston Martins worth up to £200,000 and MGAs worth at least £10,000, it would be foolish to leave a project uninsured, particularly as many classic policies can provide basic storage cover at minimal cost. Believe it or not, a repair workshop isn't bound by law to be insured for its contents and if anything happens – such as a fire or theft at the premises – then you could lose everything if your classic isn't suitably covered.

Taking out a classic car insurance policy is very wise as mainstream insurers may not provide the best protection, particularly for specialist vehicles. (MagicCarPics)

Don't think that insurance is only something you have to worry about when it's finished and ready for the road. If the vehicle is only half finished, looks scruffy and is involved in an accident, it can be marked well down in value in the eyes of the insurance assessor. I know of an enthusiast whose vehicle was involved in a prang while a repair garage was testing it and, as the vehicle's body was only half finished and looked scruffy, it was marked well down in value, meaning the owner lost big money upon pay-out and had to get it repaired at his own cost.

It is becoming increasingly common for classic owners to include their vehicle(s) on a mainstream multi-car policy. While it's convenient and perhaps cheaper, it only really makes sense with a modern classic, which may not qualify for classic insurance cover anyway. However, mainstream insurers don't understand classics like a good, well-known, experienced specialist does, which is why it's wise to chat to an old-fashioned broker first. That's another benefit of choosing a dedicated classic car policy – the chance to talk to a human being rather than being just a click on a soulless computer.

HIRING A CLASSIC

Rather than buying a classic, why not hire one instead? This practice is becoming increasingly popular as it provides most of the joys of classic motoring without the burden of running costs, such as statutory insurance, road tax, annual MOT test and any potentially costly repairs. In addition to this, there are no long-term parking or storage problems and, best of all, no purchasing outlay to drain the bank account.

On average, for less than £200 a day you can get behind the wheel of a wide variety of classics, great if you prefer the chance to savour a diversity of lovely cars. Some companies go further and provide special inclusive UK and European tours with accompanied support and guides, planned routes, packed lunches, overnight stays at chosen quality hotels with dinner and breakfast – and more.

At the other end of the scale, there's a selection of short (usually hourly) taster drives costing comfortably under £50, which allow you to test drive a representative model over varied routes. This is a brilliant way of discovering the delights of classic motoring inexpensively, and it gives enthusiasts the chance to sample a choice of classics to see which one suits them best – potentially saving them thousands by not making the wrong choice. It also offers the chance to drive a classic of your dreams – if not budget – for a short while!

There are numerous specialists in this field and the HCHG (classiccarhire.co.uk) is the UK's network of classic hire companies, with more than fifty cars on the fleet. In addition to this, a good many marque specialists (such as the The SL Shop (Mercedes) and Morgan dealers) also operate

Hiring rather than owning a classic can make a lot of sense as it enables you to sample many different makes and models, plus it relieves you of the worry and expense of maintenance and repairs. (MagicCarPics)

A classic commercial will get you noticed and promote your business or trade at the same time. However, bear in mind their comfort and performance levels will be minimal.

hire schemes. The Classic Cars Loan Project (classiccarloanproject.co.uk) offers a selection of classic cars for loan periods up to a year with the aim to encourage new, younger enthusiasts to take up the hobby.

The final decision is a personal one and rests upon whether you want to own rather than simply drive a classic car. But given that their average annual mileage is a little over 1,000 miles, hiring a classic could well be the smartest option.

CLASSIC CAR CLUBS

There's no excuse for not joining a classic car club – with around 500 regional and national associations, there's one suited for your intended classic. And for comfortably less than £1 a week they make ownership so much easier and more enjoyable. Being a member of a dedicated club brings many privileges, such as special-rate insurance, lower-cost spares and servicing, and an easy way to buy or sell a classic. Specialists really rely upon word-of-mouth recommendation for their future custom, and feedback given by members – be it positive or negative – filters back and is spread among fellow club members.

Joining a relevant owners' club is well worth your while as they can be of massive help in so many areas, plus the social side is worth the price of annual membership alone.

Expert advice from those who own and drive the same model as you is always invaluable, as they will have proven knowledge of tweaks and shortcuts that could save you money as well as trouble. Some club websites share links to videos showing in detail how to repair or fit parts. The Rolls-Royce Enthusiasts' Club, for example, goes even further and runs dedicated workshop seminars to help owners maintain their classics with confidence.

Club forums are becoming increasingly popular in providing up-to-date advice because there's nothing that cannot be resolved by posting your enquiry online and waiting for instant help. Most forums also include a section answering frequently asked questions (FAQs) on common problems. Forums are also particularly helpful at sourcing parts and loaning special tools.

The social scene alone seals it for many because lifelong friendships are frequently formed, especially as part of the clubs that attend shows and provide vibrant must-visit stands, perhaps holding live entertainment to make the day go off with a bang. Social functions are also very common and popular, from monthly get-togethers at a local pub to themed weekends away, perhaps involving a treasure hunt or suchlike.

Motor clubs need a healthy membership to survive, and it's not simply for financial reasons either because many are run by volunteers. They also require help – and this is where you might fit in. Their magazines and online sites certainly welcome fresh new features and writers, for example. Most news-stand classic magazines include a listing of all the major clubs and you won't regret joining one.

WORTHWHILE MODIFICATIONS

Even if you don't contemplate fast road driving, let alone track use, and prefer originality in the slow lane instead, there's still a good many modifications worth incorporating in a classic without risk of diluting its character at all.

Leaving out any performance mods, virtually every classic will prove more reliable and perform better with sensible upgrades, most of which are fully accepted within many owners' clubs because they enhance the vehicle in question. It gets complicated when contemplating modifications that are irreversible, and as classics get older, the desire for originality may cause problems in the future. If alterations can be successfully reversed, then there is little to worry over.

It's sadly an all-too-common sight to see old vehicles by the roadside boiling over, yet it needn't be so as they didn't overheat when new! A wise upgrade, if the cooling system needs a new radiator anyway, is to replace it with an uprated alternative, providing up to 50 per cent better heat dissipation, although just installing an electric cooling fan (along with a new thermostat) may cure many hot running worries. Another worthwhile aid is what's known as 'waterless coolant'. This is a dedicated solution that is a substitute for normal water and cannot boil or freeze. The cost to change using Evans Waterless Coolant can be around £100, but it's a fill-and-forget procedure.

Unleaded cylinder heads are a must if ever the engine is receiving an overhaul. This may have been carried out already, but don't leave it to chance as off-the-shelf fuel additives to counter the lack of lead in today's petrol are only a substitute. You can purchase a ready-to-fit cylinder head or, as most owners do, have the existing head converted using specially hardened valve seats by an overhauler for a few hundred pounds.

Electronic ignition has been standard on engines for fifty years on some classics, and it's one of the best engine modifications you can make, as many owners have discovered, for as little as £30. Replacing the normal ignition set-up with a fit-and-forget electronic module, which fits unobtrusively inside the distributor cap, ensures that the engine never falls out of tune and also improves performance, economy and emissions, although to enjoy the advantages to the full it is best to also use a higher-performance coil and ignition leads to suit.

Certain modifications, such as extra power, not only improve the driving experience but can also enhance the car's desirability and resale value.

Five-speed gearboxes (or four- or five-speed automatics) are a boon for the majority of classics, making them far less fussy and more economical on faster roads. Proper fitting kits are available for many popular classics although some (such as MGAs) may require extensive, irreversible chassis mods in order to fit the bigger transmission, so think it over beforehand. That said, many have been successfully converted either by a dedicated kit or ingenuity, transforming the drive as long as the engine has the power to 'pull' the extra gear. Sadly, this is where a good number of lower-powered classics of less than 1.5 litres, such as Ford Anglias and Morris Minors, can fall down, requiring engine uprating to obtain the full benefits of a five-speed transmission.

One of the stark differences between classics and moderns is their superior stopping power so it is wise to uprate the brakes. An owners' club or marque specialist will have advice depending upon your needs and budget, and the same is the case for suspension upgrades. Both are becoming popular modifications, as is electronic power steering, and are installations that are hard to detect but totally reversible.

Any of the above enhancements will be nullified if the tyres are substandard. Because tyres age, a new matching set will transform how your classic steers, grips and rides. You have the choice of either opting for mainstream modern types or a classic design, which was factory fitment when your classic was new. Opinions are divided on the merits and demerits of each so speak to a classic tyre specialist first.

Modifications don't always mean more speed. They can also be about conveniences such as better lighting (most oldies are miserable in this respect), heating and winter weather aids like higher-powered starters, heated windscreens, two-speed wipers and suchlike. With all this going

on, the stock dynamo (generator) on a pre-1970 car can't possibly cope so consider a swap to an alternator or a dynamo-looking Dynalite. The latter combines modern alternator technology with the appearance of an old dynamo and provides up to 80 per cent more power, it is claimed. Finally, it's best to retain all the old parts should you wish to sell your classic on to a buyer who likes your car if not the mods ...

Nothing looks more out of place in a classic than a modern in-car entertainment system. Period radios can be rebuilt with modern innards to provide the best of both worlds.

WORKING CLASSICS

A classic needn't sit idle in the garage when it can pay for itself. With an increasing number of TV programmes, films and events featuring old cars, you could make yours earn its keep as well as adding a touch of fame to its CV. Special agencies such as Action Wheels, Vehicles in Vision and Vision Motor Services are known for showing the right vehicle to the right audience, either as a standing prop or for a moving sequence. Generally the classic must be in period condition (so no alloy wheels and suchlike) and well presented. If an actor has to drive the vehicle, any little foibles – such as a sharp-acting clutch or very heavy steering – should be mentioned to the production staff. Expect to earn around £500 per day on a major production, less typically 20 per cent commission. Also, you must inform your insurance company, but usually the production company in question will provide cover.

If you have a classic as recognisable as *The Saint*'s Volvo P1800 then you could accrue some welcome extra income by loaning it out for photographic or film and TV production work. (Volvo via Newspress)

Not everybody wants a white Rolls-Royce for their big day! Novelty classics are becoming increasingly popular. Buy the right classic and you could be onto a nice little earner and have some fun at the same time.

Classic wedding hire is very common, as not everybody wants a white Rolls-Royce! You may have to be chauffeur at the same time (and need to dress accordingly). Again, the classic has to be in eye-turning condition, complete with appropriate ribbons. You can either contact hire companies and offer your services or self-advertise (perhaps via an owners' club), but do inform your insurance company as a premium is bound to be charged. Photo shoots to launch a product and celebrate a certain anniversary is another money earner, but as with any extra earnings, you must inform HM Revenue and Customs.

If you are a tradesperson then a classic commercial – even a lorry – can be a useful business partner. It will advertise your profession in a very special way, although daily use will take its toll on the vehicle's condition – and could you stand driving such a rudimentary oldie (as invariably they all were, even when new) day in, day out?

CLASSIC MOTORSPORT

Anyone who has ever attended the likes of the Goodwood Revival, Silverstone Classic and other historic events understands why and how motorsport competition brings a whole new dimension to ownership fun, harking back to the good old days when you could actually identify with the cars in action.

You may not be the next Lewis Hamilton, but don't let that stop you having immense enjoyment competing as you can use virtually any car, even in standard road-going form, in some level of competition. Best of all, you don't require a competition driving licence or medical for many disciplines as more than two-thirds of all categories don't demand one.

Before you decide on which motorsport category to excel in (racing, rallying, hill-climbing, off-roading, etc.), attend as many events as you can to get the feel of things. Speak to competitors for advice as the majority are only too willing to help. It may look easy enough but it isn't – competition driving is far removed from fast driving on the road. Specialist driving schools will help you develop the minimum skills needed, but to gain a full-blown competition licence you have to enrol in Motorsport UK approved special race and rally schools to take it further.

The beauty of classic competition is that many makes and models have their own racing championships, tailored for both standard road-legal models and full-blown competition cars so everybody can join in the fun. Most popular marques are MGs, Triumphs, Caterhams, Morgans, Minis and latterly Mazda MX-5s, Toyota MR2s and even Austin's dainty A30/A35. Many one-make classic car clubs are heavily involved in motorsport so it's a good idea to join one because usually they operate minor low-cost events for standard and modified cars, thus making them ideal for novices or those who simply want to do it for fun and aren't bothered by being at the back of the pack – unless you're an ace with pace of course!

You can compete for as little as £20 if you chose a 'lightweight' event such as autotesting or trials, but if you become more involved and competitive, the time, effort and cost can rise dramatically, especially if your classic evolves into a more race- or rally-orientated machine and requires trailering to events.

There's no shortage of second-hand competition classics for sale, but check out their specific competition history, results and inspect them as you would any old vehicle. If possible, try before you buy. But why buy at all? One-make series often provide lease racers, and it may be better to go down this route rather than own something that you also have to store, maintain and fix, especially if spares and race support are included in the package.

Motorsport brings a new dimension to classic ownership and there's a wide variety of disciplines, including one-marque racing championships such as this exclusive Alfa Romeo event. (Silverstone Classic)

Above left: Classic tours are non-competitive events but are still great fun; you have to drive with vigour while taking in some lovely roads and scenery. (MagicCarPics)
Above right: Virtually any classic can compete and there's no shortage of previously owned cars for sale. Check out their provenance and, if possible, have a track test before buying.

There's another route to consider. If you seek the thrills and experience of fast driving but without the hassle and cost of full-blown competition, consider a Track Day or its rally equivalent. These are non-competitive events generally costing from £99 per day, yet they are one of the best ways to learn about competition driving at your own pace and ability. A slow car is often easier to use for novices because you can concentrate on learning racing lines instead of having to wrestle with performance – and all its temptations. Some events have professional race/rally tutors on hand who charge a small fee to sit in the passenger seat and guide you around the circuit. Bagging a ride with other owners also helps to learn about driving around a race circuit at no cost.

There's no requirement for a competition licence (although drivers must hold a full licence) or membership, although the latter is worthwhile as these organisations may well hold special days. Costs vary between £100 for a simple airfield event to around £400 at an established prestige circuit. Most organisers require a car to be at least road legal (current MOT test certificate) and crash helmets must be worn by the driver and any passenger.

Scenic Tours are relaxing yet lively jaunts over some of the best driving roads with delightful overnight stops included. Standard classics are welcome, but obviously your car needs to be up to the job, and you'll need to take spares and so on, although some outfits can even provide top-notch classics to do the tour in.

Finally, you can be part of the action by offering your services and enthusiasm to the scene by helping out in event organisation or as a track marshal where you are actively in the thick of the competition, displaying driving warning flags where necessary and helping out after any incidents and accidents – plus enjoying the best viewing points possible at the same time! And if you like working on classics more than driving them, or are handy with the socket set, there are plenty of competitors who are in need of a good race mechanic at the weekends.

PART 2

CLASSIC HOT 100 CARS

If you have reached this stage in the book, then you are ready to pick your chosen classic. Here is a hot 100 of them (and their derivatives) that should satisfy the tastes of the majority of enthusiasts.

Each selected model includes a brief resume of the most important changes during their production run, a generally accepted appraisal of what they are like to drive, dedicated buying tips applicable to that make and model, and a guide to prices to pay for them. However, the valuations of classics are not set in stone. As with normal car prices, variables such as overall condition, provenance, desirability and current market influences will all play a part in the price asked, and only you can decide whether they represent fair value or not. Finally, each classic is given a unique, short and sharp verdict – many of which may well surprise you ...

ASTON MARTIN DB4–6

Although this trio differ in many ways, the Aston Martin DB is one of the ultimate pin-up classics thanks to its quintessential Britishness and status as the definitive James Bond car.

(Author)

DATES TO REMEMBER
1958   DB4 is a virtually all-new design with a Superleggera chassis and twin-cam 3.6-litre engine.
1960   Series 2 sees many detailed improvements plus optional overdrive.
1961   Series 3 has 'twin spark plug' 302bhp GT tune offered. Series 4 has styling alterations, and availability of Special Series engine.

1962   Longer body for Series 5, automatic transmission offered, Special Series engine now standard.

1963   DB5 succeeds DB4 and is essentially the same car apart from later 3,995cc engine.

1964   Triple Weber carb Vantage option (314bhp).

1965   DB6 has longer wheelbase and 'duck tail' boot lid for better aerodynamics.

1969   DB6 Mk2 is identified by flared wheel arches to house fatter tyres. AE Brico electronic fuel injection was optional.

DRIVING

They all perform differently. The DB4 can be called the sports car of the trio despite being the least powerful (240bhp) as, thanks its lightness and compact size, it's the most agile. The DB5 is the fastest of them all while the DB6 is the best handler, although if you have never driven these old Astons before, don't expect to find GTi precision because they are heavy beasts to manhandle. Most buyers want the Vantage tune, but experts say the triple-SU engines are best for everyday use. Automatics are universally disliked as they really sap performance, although, on the other hand, they are cheaper to buy.

BUYING TIPS

Rust and poor past repairs are the biggest worries as restoration costs are exorbitant. Condition is everything as the Superleggera build (aluminium panels over a tubular steel skeleton structure) is as complex as it is expensive and difficult to rectify. If you don't know what you are looking for then it's best to entrust a top Aston specialist or the owners' club to help you, as there are many great-looking but poorly kept cars out there. The sturdy engines can become sludged up due to their reliance on replaceable iron piston liners. A full and proper engine rebuild can run to a cool £25,000 or more.

PRICES

Condition is everything but the middle DB5 is still the clear leader as a cool half a million is needed for a good, but by no means concours, car, followed by the DB4 and DB6 at around £400,000 and £300,000 respectively. Soft-top Volantes are valued much more across the board while LHD has little impact on residuals. Don't reckon that a barn find is a sure-fire money earner as these have fetched an amazing £200,000, and you'll need this amount again to restore one properly.

VERDICT

A dream classic for many wannabe 007s, their desirability as well as exclusivity will always keep values high. This 1960s Aston is just as much about ownership satisfaction as behind-the-wheel-thrills. You get what you pay for, though.

ASTON MARTIN DBS & V8

(Historics Auctioneers)

Perhaps it was an image thing? The DBS has always trailed in the tyre tracks of the more illustrious DB predecessors, yet it survived to become Aston's longest-lived model.

DATES TO REMEMBER

1967   DBS launched, effectively a rebodied DB6 but with the de Dion rear suspension first seen in the Lagonda Rapide saloon.

1969   5.3-litre V8 introduced with Bosch fuel injection, producing 345bhp and 400lb ft of torque to supplement DBS6.

1972   Series 2 now sports new two-headlamp frontal design and, because company founder David Brown sold the ailing company, the cars are now simply known as Vantage (DBS6) and V8 respectively.

1973   Series 3 has four twin-choke Webers to replace the unreliable Bosch fuel injection. The six-cylinder car continues to be offered, known simply as the Vantage.

1977   V8 is offered in Stage I tune before a Vantage edition is introduced with 390bhp.

1978   Series 4, identified by a bonnet bulge, new dash and revised trim.

1980   Special high-compression '580' engine replaces earlier unit.

1986   Series 5 sees return of fuel injection (305bhp). Final V8 development; Vantage, in X-Specification guise, packing a rousing 410bhp.

DRIVING

While the DBS is bulkier and heavier than past DBs, its wider track and lengthened wheelbase over the DB6 result in the car feeling much more planted on the road, even if the Aston's size and heft make it more suave transcontinental GT than agile sports car. The V8 has the power the heavier DBS always needed, although the DBS6 is not as sluggish as its reputation suggests unless it's an automatic, which feels positively lazy. The DBS is certainly the more comfortable, roomier tourer than previous DBs.

BUYING TIPS

As with earlier DBs, rust and poor past repairs are the biggest obstacles even though the DBS doesn't feature Superleggera construction. Sills are a major concern and other rot spots are A/B posts, floors and the substantial box sections. If you're looking at a Volante, inspect the metal between the fuel flaps. The V8 is sturdy so long as there is 60lb oil pressure. Poor performance and low compressions point to piston-ring or value-guide wear. The six-cylinder engine is as tough, but relies on replaceable iron piston liners which can become sludged up if neglected. A full professional engine rebuild can cost more than an overhaul of the later V8. The ZF manual gearbox is not silent although it shouldn't be excessively noisy either. Being a heavy car, the steering and suspension absorbers suffer accordingly.

PRICES

Whereas a few years ago good examples of a DBS6 could be snatched up for £40,000, you'll now need to spend over £100,000 to secure something as nice, and an exceptional V8 can sell for double. Unless in top condition, DBS6 automatics are the cheapest by far due to their reputation for sluggishness, but as not many folks drive their classics flat out, their lack of pace may not be such a problem.

VERDICT

Unfairly shunned for decades, the DBS is finally enjoying the reputation it always deserved as a sleeker, roomier, more refined and palatial GT than its iconic film-star predecessors. Prices that are still attainable are the icing on the cake.

ASTON MARTIN DB7

(Newspress/Aston Martin)

An affordable Aston for the 1990s, the DB7 is often slated for being little more than a 'Jag in drag'. While the 'new DB4' is heavily XJ-S based, it still has that special Aston character.

DATES TO REMEMBER

1994   DB7 (I6) is launched, relying upon the XJ-S platform, painted by Rolls-Royce and developed by the Jaguar Le Mans winning team, Tom Walkinshaw Racing. Available initially as a coupé powered by a (Jaguar-derived) 335bhp supercharged straight-six engine.

1996   The long-anticipated convertible Volante appears with a powered hood but also a softer suspension set-up.

1997   A wealth of much-needed improvements are dialled in, including better build quality.

1999   V12-engined DB7 launched under the Vantage label, with a 6-litre 420bhp unit that is essentially two Ford Mondeo V6s 'married' together, and is also offered in both coupé and Volante forms.

2002   Special run-out models on sale such as the GT, complete with an uprated V12 and suspension tweaks.

2003   Final fling came when the Zagato-bodied Vantage Volante was unveiled. Tenth anniversary normal DB7s were also built just before the DB9 came along.

DRIVING

Perhaps the DB7 doesn't drive quite as brilliantly as it looks, but it's still an accomplished GT that feels far more modern than any Aston before it. It wasn't until the V12-engined Vantage of 1999 that the virtually re-engineered DB7 finally came of age, although there are those who feel that the earlier 'supercharged six' gives the Aston a more thoroughbred feel. Hitting almost 160mph and passing the 60mph mark in under 6 seconds is quick enough for most, although the V12 takes it to another level. The DB7's handling isn't as sportingly sharp as a Porsche 911 but satisfying enough, and keen enthusiasts will find that the stiffer-shelled coupés hold a handling advantage over the convertibles.

BUYING TIPS

With some 7,000 made there's little shortage so try as many as possible, as they will vary. As the DB7 is essentially a Jaguar, it can be serviced by most normal garages, but the major services should be done by a marque specialist. DB7s can fail the annual MOT due to rust and, if anything, the later cars suffer the most because Aston skimped on underseal and, by 2002, had stopped rust-proofing their cars completely! Both engines are robust if serviced properly. Watch for odd tyre wear and be aware that the suspension geometry is probably maladjusted and V12 wheel rims can give problems.

PRICES

Not so long ago you could pick up a DB7 for under £15,000; now top-model prices surpass those of the later V8 Vantage and DB9. The bottom line is around £20,000 for a very average 'six', rising to £35,000 for a top model. On average, Volantes are valued around £5,000 more, and you can add £10,000 on top of all these prices for V12s, with the GT/GTA ticketed at as much as £70,000 if concours.

VERDICT

Perhaps the DB7 is more Johnny English than James Bond, but its Jaguar lineage doesn't take anything away from this Aston Martin and they are still good value for money and much cheaper to run than any previous DB.

ALVIS TD-TF

(Author)

This overlooked upper-crust English carmaker offers Bentley-like prestige and pedigree, Rolls-Royce quality, Bristol exclusivity plus a unique detached air of dignity.

DATES TO REMEMBER

1956 TC108G launched: basically a TC21 redesigned by Swiss coachbuilder Graber.

1958 Now badged TD21 after a refresh by Park Ward, the new model is identified by a single-piece rear window.

1959 Front disc brakes now fitted as standard to cope with a power increase to 115bhp. Automatic transmission is now an option.

1960 Another subtle body makeover, plus the Austin-Healey-sourced manual gearbox gains an overdrive option for better cruising.

1962 Series 2 is equipped with rear disc brakes. A five-speed ZF manual is now available to special order.

1963 The TE21 upgrade is easily identified by its novel stacked quad headlight styling, plus the engine is uprated to 130bhp.

1965 Power steering becomes optional.

1966 TF bolstered with special tuned triple-carb 150bhp engine and uprated suspension and also features a different dashboard design.

DRIVING

Alvis made some of the best grand tourers in coupé and cabriolet guises during their day, with comfort and space to spare, providing refinement that would do a similar aristocratic Rolls or Bentley proud. While not exactly road burners, compared to a compatible Jaguar XK or Aston Martin DB2, the TD–TF can hold their own with surprisingly able handling for a car weighing some 1.5 tonnes, although with period roads tests reporting 0–60mph times of 12–14 seconds, performance from these heavyweights isn't that notable. But at the same time, when you drive an Alvis you quickly realise that outright speed isn't everything.

BUYING TIPS

Only 784 examples of the Series 1 TD21 and 289 versions of the Series 2 were made. Just over 350 TE21s and a mere 106 TF21s were produced, meaning it may just be a case of what you can get. But like-for-like the last of the line TE/TF are best due to their superior running gear, such as power steering, disc brakes and so on. Specialist support from Red Triangle is excellent, and they even make reproduction models (at a cost) so spares are not really a problem (although prices may be with new wings priced at £1,800 apiece). Build quality was top notch and the strong chassis is durable, but watch for rot in the box sections and suspension points. The mechanicals, which come from a variety of contemporary car makers, are similarly robust, although a full engine overhaul is likely to run to £10,000. Similarly, the Rolls-like interior is costly to renovate.

PRICES
Until the last five years an Alvis represented spectacular value for money, but as enthusiasts cottoned on to this fact values have risen sharply of late, but are still well below that of a Jaguar XK and perhaps a tenth that of an Aston DB2. You can own a tidy coupé for well under £40,000.

VERDICT
A classic for the real connoisseur who wishes to keep a low profile. Loved by royalty and A-list celebs of that time for the car's impeccable taste and breeding, what's not to like, and all for the price of a Triumph TR6?

ALFA ROMEO SPIDER

Alfa Romeo's Spider enjoyed a production run spanning three decades. This means you can own a classic without the usual old car age-related hang-ups.

DATES TO REMEMBER
1966   New Alfa sports car has sophisticated spec: twin-cam engine, five-speed transmission and all-round disc brakes.
1967   1.6-litre engine grows to 1,750cc to create the Spider Veloce, today regarded by many as the sweetest and most desirable model out of the range.
1968   1.3-litre Spider Junior joins the line-up.
1970   Original distinctive boat tail rear end gives way to a square-cut Kamm-tail look.
1971   2-litre Spider Veloce takes over from the 1750, while a 1600 Junior joins the ranks for 1972.
1978   UK imports end.

1983   LHD only Series 3 sporting wider tyres, body kit, redesigned rear lamps and rubber bumpers as standard plus an ungainly looking boot spoiler.

1990   A final facelift by Pininfarina sees a return to the original looks and official UK imports restart until production finally ends in April 1993.

DRIVING

Thanks to its advanced design, the Spider has always remained entertaining to drive and a world away from an MGB with rev-happy engines, sporting gearing and predictable rear-wheel-drive handling. The later S3/S4 cars kept abreast of the times with fuel injection, power steering and more safety kit, yet still retained much of the original character, although cars from the US with their detuned engines and softer suspension are not so nice.

BUYING TIPS

Being Italian, rust is always the main concern in just about every nook and cranny. It's reckoned that S2 cars are best served for parts; boat-tailed and S3 cars the least, with some panels almost extinct. In the US (where 75 per cent of all Spiders were destined for) cars may be free from rot. As the engines are physically identical, apart from their capacities, many have upgraded to a larger size. This is not a problem, except for the fact that there are differences in gearings, while the 1300 used an inferior brake set-up. The 2000 engines can suffer from head and head-gasket woes while fuel injection (Bosch or the earlier Spica) can be unreliable but easily sorted by experts.

PRICES

With a car spanning three decades there's something for everybody. Predictably the later S3/S4 versions are the cheapest, the former in particular which are easy £5,000 buys, but the S4 is far preferable for an extra £2,500 meaning £10,000 tops. There's a big jump to S2 ownership where £20,000+ isn't uncommon and this can easily double for the boat-tailed models.

VERDICT

Like Dustin Hoffman, isn't it time you considered graduating to a true thoroughbred sports car? Why not one which was on par with the Lotus Elan in its day and streets ahead of our MGB or Triumph TR, and so still feels relatively modern?

ALFA ROMEO GTV AND GIULIA

(Author)

Alfa Romeo is very probably the closest marque you can get to an affordable Italian supercar, which enjoy classic status and yet can remain surprisingly affordable.

DATES TO REMEMBER

1962/3 105 Series Giulia 1600 Ti/Super saloon is launched, followed by Giulia Sprint GT coupé.

1966 1300 GTV Junior is added to the range.

1967 Engine size grows to 1,750cc to create the legendary 1750 GTV. Also a 94bhp 1300 Giulia saloon is introduced.

1968 Giulia 1750 saloon joins ranks.

1972 2000 GTV and 2000 Berlina saloon introduced featuring 132bhp engine and a limited-slip differential. 1600 Junior Spider, along the lines of the earlier 1300, joins the ranks. Changes include a revised grille especially on the 2000GTV. The 1300 and 1600 versions wore singular headlamps but in their final years also gained 2000GTV look.

1974 Berlina (Giulia) saloon finally gains option of automatic transmission. Like the GTV, both are discontinued in 1977, but for the UK market there was a dedicated SE model complete with a vinyl roof and tinted glass.

DRIVING

Thanks to the forward design and specification for their era, Alfas still feel something special by today's standards, largely due to their sparkling engines, even the gallant little 1300. GTVs have all the style, but the boxy Giulia saloons drive equally well yet are as practical as a Cortina. They are also much cheaper, although bear in mind that the very earliest sported column gearchanges and drum brakes.

BUYING TIPS

As with any 1960s Alfa, ruinous rust is the first checkpoint – just about anywhere. Some late GTVs were fitted with a factory vinyl roof, which was 'tacked' in place and if the covering is removed, you can see the holes left! A healthy engine will register 50–70lb oil pressure but can drop to almost zero at idle. Cylinder head gaskets can be worrisome, with the 2000 head known for cracking in particular. Weber Dellorto and Solex carbs were employed and all are very expensive to overhaul. Gearboxes are okay, although synchro on second is prone to fail. Axles are long-lasting, but the limited-slip diff on 2000s (and some 1750s) requires special tools and expert knowledge to repair. Trim parts, for saloons mainly, are now difficult to source.

PRICES

Bargain hunters should look at the saloons, or better still the later Berlina, where average-to-good cars are available at under £5,000. In comparison, the greatest of Giulias can sell for four times as much! GTVs are considerably pricier with the best models valued at £40–50,000 depending on model, although you should deduct in the region of £10,000 for most Juniors. That said, anyone after any coupé needs to spend at least £15,000 for anything half decent.

VERDICT

A great range of classy classics boasting one of the most evocative badges on the block, yet they can be surprisingly attainable and affordable if you look at the left-field and left-hand-drive variants. The time to buy is now.

ALFA ROMEO GTV AND SPIDER (916)

New millennium replacements for the iconic GTV and Spider have all the style and sophistication that you'd expect from Alfa Romeo. The V6 models are genuine junior supercars.

DATES TO REMEMBER

1996   Introduced (just after the Fiat Coupé), both on a shared Fiat Tipo-based platform. Alfa engines are employed starting with the well-proven 150bhp 2-litre Twin Spark (two spark plugs per cylinder). Trims are Lusso or Turismo on both GTV and Spider.

1997   V6 engine joins range; a 220bhp 3-litre 24V unit, complemented by bigger Brembo brakes and special 16in 'teledial' wheels.

1998   Phase II facelift involves minor exterior and interior changes. Six-speed manual transmission option for V6 while the 2-litre engine's power is raised slightly to 155bhp.

2001   GTV Cup special edition has V6 engine and special body kit; eighty were issued for the UK. Numerous run-out special editions for 2002.

2003   Phase II revision featured bigger tyres and small styling refresh. Mechanically, the engines are up-gunned: 163bhp for the 2-litre 'JTS' and 237bhp for the enlarged 3.2-litre V6.

DRIVING

In spite of its front-wheel-drive, Fiat Tipo hatchback underpinnings, the Alfa manages to carve out a character of its own as a modern classic with some old-school soul, although the similar Fiat Coupé is the better driving car despite the Alfa's dedicated rear-suspension design. The fixed-head GTVs are the best handlers, as the roofless high-style Spiders can feel somewhat wishy-washy. If anything, the four-cylinder variants have the edge on handling because the superb 3-litre V6 is sadly noted for its excessive understeer as well as an inferior ride. But what an engine it is, developing at least 220bhp and almost 240bhp in later six-speed 3.2 tune, enjoying Ferrari-like sounds and sensations.

BUYING TIPS

Thanks to fully galvanised bodies, rust isn't too much of a problem, although front subframe rot isn't unknown and rectification may outweigh the value of some cars. Mechanically, ensure the cambelt has been replaced when recommended, and beware of variable-valve-timing problems. The Alfa's chassis has a sophisticated suspension set-up, but the downside is that when it goes wrong, it's bad news. Does the car come with all the keys? It's important as a missing 'master key' can cost about £1,000 to replace as the engine's ECU may require changing as a result.

PRICES

For those after something a cut above the rest on a tight budget, these classy Alfas tick all the right boxes and it's hard to find a better prestige sports classic for the money. You can pick up a fair GTV or Spider for under £2,000 and even the best V6s can't exceed £7,000.

VERDICT

Arguably, despite their Fiat parentage, they are the last of the true Alfa Romeos. That said, it's worth taking a hard look at the later GT Coupé and Brera replacements, which are just as inexpensive and becoming sought after.

AUDI QUATTRO

(Author)

Quattro is the car and concept that changed our perception of all-wheel drive for ever and spawned a family of Quattros in saloon, coupé, cabriolet and estate guises.

DATES TO REMEMBER

1980   Introduced, based upon a Volkswagen 4x4 set-up (designed for the military) in razor-edged coupé guise and powered by a 200bhp 2.2-litre, five-cylinder engine. Initially the car was only available in LHD.

1982   Significant chassis changes saw tweaks to the rear suspension while the transmission diff locks were upgraded at the same time. Externally, single headlamps were installed in favour of the original quad style.

1983   More revisions included the standard fitting of Bosch anti-lock brakes and larger Ronal alloys while the suspension was lowered by 20mm. To give an all-round sportier feel, the gear ratios were revised.

1988   Audi gave the Quattro a new lease of life with a new MB engine, with a smaller turbo for better throttle response, better brakes and a Torsen torque-sensing differential for the 4x4 system, allowing an automatic grip split.

1989   Punchier twin-cam 20V tune introduced, derived from the Sport Quattro.

DRIVING

It says something that forty years on, the Quattro still cuts it on modern roads with the best performance cars and remains one of the most practical performance cars ever made. Quattros suffer from a ludicrous turbo lag, but that's all part of the 1980s character, yet despite the performance, you can see fuel returns in the mid 20s. Handling grip was outstanding in its day, but that was more due to the 4x4 system as the chassis was deemed average. This was especially the case in the earliest cars, which suffered strong, albeit safe, understeer. Later cars boasting the Torsen differential, instead of the original fixed 50/50 transmission split, are much better and certainly Quattros featuring anti-lock brakes are far preferable.

BUYING TIPS

Officially there are 163 LHD UK registered cars. The first chassis number for RHD model was 85DA900556. As with all rare performance cars, an independent check by an Audi specialist is money well spent. A VW/Audi parts bin special, Quattros are pretty easy to maintain, even though parts supply is patchy, and there are specialists around to contain costs although Quattro servicing is invariably dearer than a mainstream Quattro. They were almost hand-made, but pre-1985 bodies weren't galvanised and as a result rust the most. Engine rebuilds are costly; most troublesome is the 10-valve 2.2 but the MB unit is far more durable.

PRICES

There's something for everyone. Top Quattro Sport versions, of which only 214 were made, command Aston DB5-like prices, but mainstream Quattros can be bought for well under £2,000. Uber Quattros fit somewhere in-between; the dearest are 20V models which range from £40,000 to £60,000, but earlier cars are notably less expensive – say £20,000.

VERDICT

A modern motoring milestone and yet still a surprisingly affordable icon at the same time, the Audi Quattro is not only a nailed-on classic but it can also be used as a dependable and practical daily driver whatever the weather.

AUDI R8

(Author)

If you have ever longed for a supercar but are put off by their high prices and running costs, Audi's brilliant R8 may be the perfect answer as above all else, it is a sensible supercar.

DATES TO REMEMBER

2007 Launched as a 4.2-litre 420bhp V8-powered, mid-engined two-seater coupé.

2008 Lamborghini Gallardo V10 engine becomes optional, which despite being detuned still pumps out 517bhp. Previous magnetic damping is standard. Convertible Spyder is announced (2009).

2010 Hard-core 552bhp GT Coupé heads range. V8 is uprated to 424bhp.

2012 Facelift sees revised look. Mechanically S Tronic supersedes R Tronic semi auto. Range topper is new 5.2-litre V10 Plus. All new R8 for 2015.

DRIVING

Mid- rather than rear-engined, and yet one of the best ways to imagine what an R8 is like to drive is to think of a 911 but without the rough edges – and perhaps character. Unless you're very silly, this Audi won't do anything nasty, although by the same token, such clinical efficiency that Audi is famed for means the R8 doesn't provide the same adrenaline rush or driver involvement that goes with a 911. Although the latest V10s can pump out a staggering 630bhp, the original 420bhp, 4.2 litre V8 provides more than supercar pace with 60mph up in well under 6 seconds. In addition to this, some R8 pundits actually believe that this lighter engine gives the model better balanced handling. The vast majority are semi-automatic in some form. Initially, it was R tronic before the superior, faster-acting, seven-speed S tronic replaced it, but a rare manual is lovely.

BUYING TIPS

Despite being over a decade old there's little to worry about when buying, plus you can purchase an extended manufacturer's warranty on many older versions. Servicing is typically £500–£1,000 depending upon schedule. The major worry is the R8's complex aluminium body make-up because repairs are specialist and costly. The engines are inherently strong, but clutches on manuals cost £1,000 in parts alone. Suspension wear needs budgeting carefully as the wishbones are priced at some £3,000, with the magnetic dampers £800 a go.

PRICES

R8s will surely soar in value over time, yet at the moment the majority are still depreciating due to their modern status. But the value is certainly there, with early V8 models slipping under the £35,000 barrier and unlikely to become significantly cheaper. Budget on spending in the £50-£70,000 region for a later 2015/16 model. Coupés are the cheapest. There's a wealth of options and personalisation packs, which, while desirable, shouldn't jack the prices up too much.

VERDICT

Loosely based upon the Lamborghini Gallardo (with VW owning both brands), the Audi is by no means a poor substitute. If the R8 lacks one thing, it's perhaps that it doesn't quite have the wow factor or pedigree of a Lamborghini.

AUSTIN-HEALEY SPRITE

(Historics Auctioneers)

If you thought that speed was an essential part of sports-car ownership then you don't know the original Austin-Healey Sprite, better known as the Frogeye because of its cheeky face.

DATES TO REMEMBER

1958   MkI is launched. Essentially the car is based around the Austin A35 saloon but with a tuned 42.5bhp 948cc engine, plus it inherited the Morris Minor's excellent rack-and-pinion steering. It's also the first British sports car to feature monocoque construction rather than a separate chassis.

1960   Previously optional proper side screens are standard fare in place of the previous side curtains. In little more than a year, however, the Frogeye would be defunct, replaced by the more 'normal looking' Sprite MkII, also available as the Mk1 MG Midget.

1985-89 The Frogeye Car Company builds 130 glass-fibre-bodied cars utilising period mechanicals, although many ended up being fitted with more modern Midget running gear. Originality issues aside, they can fetch anywhere between £10,000 and £15,000.

DRIVING

Weighing in at little more than half a ton, it's small wonder that the Sprite feels amazingly agile and zippy for something with less than 45bhp to play with, although stark stopwatch times show it's desperately slow by modern standards – easily improved, it must be said, and many have been. The fun part of the crazy frog is cross-country motoring where the pin-sharp Frogeye handles even better than the later models, but at the same time the penalty for such go-kart-like handling is a rough ride and virtually zero civility.

BUYING TIPS

First, let's consider originality. Because the design is as basic as it can be, the A-H lends itself to improvements and modifications, such as more power, front disc brakes and so on. As a rule, they make the car better for today's roads but the Frogeye's rarity means that the closer it stays to showroom spec, the better the car's future value. Sprites of all ages rot everywhere, but chief culprits lurk underneath. That huge bonnet costs around £3,000, and is where a good deal of the car's value rests, although fibreglass replacements are available. Happily, new high-quality steel Wheeler and Davies Frogeye bodyshells are available from Classicarco. The A35 engine is peculiar to the Mk1 Sprite, plus the carburettors are rare 1⅛in versions; later 1¼in units are often substituted. Not many still use their original 948cc engine (serial number begins with 9C-U-H). Gearboxes are inherently noisy but not excessively so. Front-suspension trunnion wear is common.

PRICES

Frogeye values have shot up over the past couple of years to the point where a merely decent car with an all-steel body will now cost a whopping £20,000 at least, with rough projects perhaps priced at five figures if complete. Cars tuned in period fetch a premium so look out for names such as Donald Healey Motor Company, BMC Special Tuning, Alexander, Nerus or Speedwell parts on the car.

VERDICT

A great back-to-basics fun sports classic that's cheap to run if not to buy. You do increasingly need to keep a watchful eye on the car's originality and authenticity during your ownership due to rarity and ever-soaring values.

AUSTIN-HEALEY

(Author)

If your idea of a classic sports car is something that needs a firm hand to show it who's boss, then the brutish raw and rustic Big Healey is right up your street.

DATES TO REMEMBER

1953   Launched as 100/4, the first Big Healey (BN1) uses 2.6-litre Austin Atlantic hardware. The first hand-built cars are made in aluminium at the Healey factory; steel-bodied cars were Jensen made.

1954   A raft of changes centred on the suspension and brakes; Austin of England motifs replace the Healey ones.

1955   Bigger brakes and new four-speed gearbox with overdrive. Higher performance 100M is based upon 1953 Le Mans racer spec with 110bhp engine and uprated suspension. Officially 601 were made, but as it was a kit, many have been converted over the years.

1956	Four-cylinder 100/4 becomes 100/6 (BN3) care of 102bhp six-cylinder Austin Westminster engine and a longer wheelbase chassis.
1959	3000 MkI (BN7 or BT7 for 2+2 version) replaces 100/6, featuring a 124bhp 2,912cc C-series engine and standard front disc brakes.
1961/62	Triple SU carb model (BN7), identified by a vertically slatted front grille.
1962	BJ7 reverts to simpler twin carbs.
1964	MkIII packs 148bhp and interior gains a walnut dash.

DRIVING

Don't automatically think that the six-cylinder cars are the best, because, if anything, the lighter and more agile 100/4 is the driver's choice and prices reflect this. What the first 100/4 always lacked was a proper gearbox as it used a curious three-speed with two-speed overdrive. Handling is what you'd expect of a rudimentary 1950s sports car twinned with the minimum of refinement, heavy controls and tremendous heat soak into the cockpit, but that's all part of the car's character, as is an ultra-low ride height that is prone to wipe out the exhausts over speed bumps.

BUYING TIPS

Rust is the main deal-breaker. The chassis can corrode badly; check integrity by jacking up the car and watching the door and panel gaps shift. New frames are available from A.H. Spares and cost around £3,500, although it's a mammoth swap-over. DIY restoration is hard as the body is complicated to get right. Mechanically as strong as an ox, but if the steering feels loose it's probably because of worn kingpins.

PRICES

100/4s are appreciably the dearest with £65–70k the norm, perhaps nudging six figures for a concours example, with authentic 100Ms coming in at double this. There's a definite split with the 'sixes' and the 100/6 can be, on average, two-thirds the cost of a 3000, the exceptions being the rare 'Longbridge' models and the fifty-off production special conversion for motorsport purposes. Expect these to sell for the price of 3000s, which are pitched slightly below 100/4 values, all except for the BN7 models.

VERDICT

Without wishing to be labelled sexist, the best way to sum up a hairy Healey is to say it's an old-fashioned 'bloke's car' that's backed by an excellent network of specialists and owners' clubs. Don't discount a bargain priced 100/6.

BENTLEY MULSANNE/ ROLLS-ROYCE SILVER SPIRIT

(Author)

The car that gave Bentley its long-overdue own identity can be absurdly inexpensive to buy and run if you do it the right way.

DATES TO REMEMBER

1980   Launched in tandem with the Rolls-Royce Silver Spirit, both are largely based upon Shadow II.

1982   Turbo joins the Mulsanne range packing no less than a 50 per cent power hike, needing a retuned chassis and suspension to cope.

1984   Eight is an 'affordable' entry model with slightly less luxury and glitz.

1985   Hard-core Turbo R tops range with 324bhp.

1987   Fuel injection along with standard anti-lock brakes. Mulsanne S added enjoying the firmer suspension of the sportier R models but in easier-going non-Turbo tune.

1988   Power outputs are upped on all.

1990   Series 2 Mulsanne and Spirit ranges benefit from revised styling and automatic ride control.

1992   Four-speed automatic, sportier Brooklands replaces the old Eight.

1993   Third generation Mulsanne gains more power and improved rear seating.

1995   Park Ward limousine joins the range. Silver Spirit is updated. Turbo fitment to the LWB Silver Spur creates the Flying Spur.

1996   Ultimate Turbo R Sport.

1997   400bhp RT is special run-out model; only 50 made.

DRIVING

Even though the Mulsanne is tighter to drive than the T2 it replaced, you still don't so much drive one as get wafted along. A standard Mulsanne is about as quick as a modern family hatchback, in contrast to the Turbos which sport an Aston-like character. The Turbo R (which stands for Roadholding) is the most thrilling, but if speed isn't vital, the simpler, cheaper and easier-to-own non-turbo Brooklands (and the later S versions) also enjoy the tighter Turbo chassis set-up. The flip side is a most un-Rolls-like ride and lack of refinement. If the latter is something you must have, then opt for a Silver Spirit.

BUYING TIPS

A solid service history is critical. A £3,000 service of the complete hydraulic system, which controls the brakes and self-levelling suspension, is part of the routine maintenance schedule and, due to cost, the most neglected service item. As you'd expect, the panel gaps and paint finish should be spot on, although the bodies can rust badly – and terminally. Beware of missing or damaged brightwork and shabby interiors, as replacements can be dear. Post-1986 cars were not built up to the usual Rolls-Royce standard.

PRICES

Bargain Bentleys are aplenty as you can easily bag one for comfortably under £10,000, but whether you'd be wise to is questionable as they are very much at the bottom of the barrel. It's wiser to budget £10,000 minimum for a mainstream Mulsanne worth having. Double this for the Turbo, with Turbo Rs adding at least £10,000 to the bill if really good and original, although watch for customisation cars which can devalue it. If anything, original, well-kept Silver Spirits are now starting to attract a serious following.

VERDICT

Prestige for pennies, their feeling of well-being and owner satisfaction, together with an unrivalled sense of occasion, is second to none. Try a few as they will vary.

BENTLEY CONTINENTAL

Much more than merely a Mulsanne coupé, the Continental is a clever mix of traditional Bentley values and craftsmanship to appeal to a new type of buyer.

DATES TO REMEMBER

1991   New high-style Bentley coupé (R) carries on the Continental line based around the Turbo R Mulsanne but uses a cut-down floorpan and an interior unique to the car.

1993   Slight power hike in line with third-gen Turbo saloon coupled to a new four-speed automatic. Twin airbags and redesigned seats are part of the cabin refresh.

1995   New ZYTEK engine-management system. Traction control is now standard along with larger 17in wheels. Azure convertible launched, based upon Continental R but with milder 360bhp.

1997   Continental T introduced armed with a special 4in-shorter wheelbase and flared wheel arches. Mechanical changes include 420bhp engine tune and an uprated suspension to cope.

1999   Glamorous sun-seeking SC (Sedanca Coupé) features a novel twin-panel glass sunroof and unique sports seats.

2006   Azure switches over to Arnage platform.

DRIVING

This car enjoys two temperaments. On the one hand, the Continental drives pretty much like the Mulsanne it is based upon, while on the other, its added vim and a sportier chassis make it a viable alternative to any Aston Martin with similar grunt but more quality, comfort and kudos at less cost. If there is a drawback, it's down to the shorter wheelbases and firmer suspension, which give rise to more coarseness over any previous Bentley, and the coupé body restricts rear seat space.

BUYING TIPS

Continental checkpoints are broadly similar to the Mulsanne, although, as they are invariably driven harder, it's best to try a few to set a yardstick, as hard-used ones can feel floppy with shot suspensions and worn brakes. Some form of service history is a must. Rust shouldn't be a major issue, but, as with the saloon, subframe, mounts, floors, inner wings, bulkheads and the boot floor sills are all rot prone. On the SC, check for dampness and floor rot. Underneath, inspect the subframe, mounts, floors, inner wings, bulkheads and the boot floor. The SC gained the nickname 'soggy carpets' due to leaky roofs so check for wetness and ruined trim.

PRICES

The cheapest Continentals carry a price of £25,000 upwards, depending upon condition. Bentley specialists say £35–50,000 is the ballpark for R and T models with the best knocking on for six figures, while good SCs comfortably exceed this already. The post-1995 cars, with their superior engine-management system and other improvements, are the best buys. Azure prices start from £60,000.

VERDICT

Whether or not the Continental warrants such a price hike over the more accommodating saloon is up for you to decide, but compared to an equivalent Aston Martin they look like brilliant British bulldog bargains.

BENTLEY CONTINENTAL GT

This is the most contentious Continental because it's essentially a Volkswagen under that shapely skin, but what isn't in question is this GT's greatness and value for money.

DATES TO REMEMBER

2003 New Continental GT supersedes previous Mulsanne-based coupé but now using Volkswagen and Audi mechanicals not dissimilar to VW's 6-litre, twin-turbo, V12 Phaeton but higher powered: 552bhp/500lb ft torque.

2005 GTC drophead and longer-wheelbase Flying Spur saloon introduced.

2007 Limited-run specials introduced, such as the 'Speed' models providing 600bhp and 553lb ft of muscle; Diamond Series stops via special carbide brake discs.

2012 New range sees a twin-turbo, 4-litre, V8 option still good for 500bhp.

DRIVING

Whether or not the GT is a real Bentley is subjective but it certainly feels far more modern than its Mulsanne-based predecessor. Being all-wheel drive (like an Audi Quattro) is far more stable, feeling absolutely planted to the road and well up to the power it has to harness. A GT is ridiculously fast (0–60mph coming in under 5 seconds with a 198mph top speed) and yet is also ridiculously easy to drive fast. It is an iron fist in a velvet glove personified, even though early models lacked the usual refinement you expect from the badge. Ride can become pretty jarring as well and tyre noise is absurdly loud for a Bentley, especially with the must-have 20in wheels fitted, but really, what an affordable supercar the GT makes.

BUYING TIPS

Not every independent Bentley specialist will work on the GT due to its complexity, and as prices have tumbled, owners with bigger aspirations than pockets have found that they can't afford to run one, so look for slipshod or broken servicing schedules. Apart from the ignition-coil packs, the engine is reliable, as is the 4x4 system, although with so many sensors and relays, fault finding is complex and expensive. Don't dismiss seemingly trivial faults either, as they are usually costly to rectify. For instance, a defective starter motor requires engine removal to replace.

PRICES

GT's have stopped free falling in value, but you can still pick up a decent one for £20–25,000 – anything drastically cheaper should be viewed with suspicion. The improved 2008 line-up is available from around £45,000, which is slightly above what the first convertibles sell for. Speeds don't command hugely greater values, but certain options will boost residuals and desirability. Speak to a specialist or owners' club for advice.

VERDICT

If you can live with the WAG image, the GT is a fantastic modern supercar classic representing incredible value for money. However, it's vital that you buy on condition not price as running costs are crippling.

BENTLEY ARNAGE
(GREEN AND RED LABEL)

One common design that shared the same qualities, even if they wore two different names and characters. Deciding what car you want has to be your first priority.

DATES TO REMEMBER

1998   A right royal carve up between Volkswagen and BMW sees the brands split for the first time. Basically VW buys the brands but BMW still holds the licence to Rolls' trademark name and badge. VW, in return for still making cars at the famous Crewe works, sells the legendary R-R grille and mascot to BMW. The Bentley Arnage initially used BMW's twin-turbo BMW 4.4-litre V8, while the Silver Seraph is fitted with BMW's 5.4-litre V12, but apart from this they are identical.

1999   Bentleys rebranded as the Arnage Green and Red Label, the first using the BMW engine with the Red reverting to the familiar but reworked 400bhp 6.75-litre pushrod R-R V8.

2001   A long-wheelbase Seraph appears while Bentley remembers its Le Mans history with a special edition.

2002   Long-wheelbase version of the Red Label is offered together with the Arnage T.

2003 Extra-long RL goes on sale with 450bhp.

2006 The long-standing V8 is heavily re-engineered and stretched to 6,761cc complete with new turbochargers, resulting in an added 50bhp. To handle this, a six-speed ZF auto box is installed in 2007.

2008 Run-out models are called Final Series with a rousing 500bhp under the bonnet.

DRIVING

Looks are deceptive, for while the two models look similar they enjoy vastly different personalities. As with the Spirit/Mulsanne, the Rolls-Royce offers the most refinement with a lovely interior, but the Bentley is the more sporty. Out of the two 'Labels' the T is the harder core and specialists say buyers should try all variants to ensure they make the right choice, but Bentleys will always be the enthusiasts' choice.

BUYING TIPS

The Arnage and Seraph can almost be treated as two distinct models because the buyer who wants one of them probably won't want the other, so try them all to see what suits you best. Like the Continental GT, all are hugely complex cars. The sophisticated BMW V8 and V12 engines are durable but require expert knowledge. The bodies are beautiful, although rusty wheel arches are not uncommon on the earliest examples.

PRICES

If you want the most metal for your money, this is the car. Costing £150,000 new, you see cars at auction sell for a tenth of this, and even respected specialists (which is the best place to buy one) will relieve you of less than £30,000 for a guaranteed car, with the Seraph usually the cheaper option. On the other hand, Arnage Ts are already seen as modern classics and so it's not unknown to see them advertised for £50,000 or above.

VERDICT

Superb modern classics which are currently selling for chips and so worth buying and hanging on to. The Bentley 'Labels' are a nicer and classier alternative to a Continental GT, but don't discount the Rolls-Royce Seraph either.

BMW Z3

(Author/BMW)

If you're after a modern sports classic that isn't a Mazda MX-5, BMW's Z3 makes a fine alternative, providing retro looks and an expansive range to suit all drivers and budgets, and is a highly affordable classic BMW.

DATES TO REMEMBER

1995   Introduced; roadster based upon earlier BMW 3-Series Compact platform with four-cylinder, 140bhp, 1.9-litre power and a choice of manual or automatic transmissions. By the end of the year, a six-cylinder, 192bhp, 2.8-litre engine is added.

1998   Flagship M Roadster and Coupé arrive with 321bhp M3 engine and reworked chassis and suspension.

2000   Engines revised: a 231bhp 3.0-litre replaces the old 2.8 and a 170bhp 2.2 supersedes the original 2-litre engine.

2001   Special 2.2 and 3.0 Sport Roadsters boast sports suspension, bigger tyres on 17in alloys and interior upgrade. Uprated Z3 M Coupé features 338bhp E46 M3 power.

DRIVING

Although enjoyable enough, the Z3 is a mix of good and not so sparkling, and the BMW (M3 Roadster excepted) certainly isn't as sporty as an MX-5, and this is chiefly down to the old skittish Compact suspension set-up employed. It's not that bad, to be fair, and you may find it perfectly acceptable, and the Z3 is one of the best sports cars to tour in because it is as easy and refined to drive as a normal 3 Series. With engines spanning 1.8-litres to 3.2-litres, performance varies from spritely to searing, but all are typically BMW smooth and sweet, with the six-cylinder units providing really strong performance yet with containable economy – the best all-rounder being the 2.2. Some Z3s also come with a four-speed automatic option.

BUYING TIPS

Despite being a modern, early Z3s can suffer serious rust problems. It's usually cosmetic but can be severe at the rear where rot attacks the diff and subframe mount areas, requiring costly welding as the axle has to be removed first. A service history increases in importance in relation to the car's price. Water-pump impeller and head-gasket failures are common to all engines, while six-cylinder engines need a watch for their Nikasil bore coating wearing, leading to smoking, poor performance, etc. plus failing VANOS valve-timing systems. Disc brake and calliper corrosion are not uncommon, too. Interiors can look tatty if neglected and the seats can rattle in their runners, but there are aftermarket bushes to cure this.

PRICES

Z3s can be spectacular value for money and you often see them for sale for under £1,000, but it's best to spend more (say £3,000) on a good rot-free example with service history. By and large, the engine size doesn't influence values all that much, the exception being the Z3 Roadster where top ones can nudge £20,000, and its Coupé alternative can run up to well over £30,000 due to its rarity and an increasingly healthy following.

VERDICT

The cultured Z3 is a serious sports car, which is as easy to drive and run as a 3-Series saloon and a worthy alternative to the seemingly default choice of a Mazda MX-5. Why not try one before deciding to see what suits you best?

BMW 3 SERIES

A most sought-after second-hand car, the 3 Series also has a classic touch about it irrespective of model or era. Apart from being fine drives they are practical and easy to own.

DATES TO REMEMBER

1975   First 3 Series (E21) generation launched initially as the four-cylinder 1.6 316 and 2-litre 320, the latter engine also available with fuel injection, boosting power from 109bhp to 125bhp before becoming a 'six' not long after.

1977   A new six-cylinder (M60) engine for the carb-fed 320 but 320i is replaced with new range-topping 2.3-litre 323i. Later, a mid-range 1.8-litre 318 joins the fray.

1983   E30 replacement retains similar appearance, albeit it with smoother lines and now a four-door option, but is significantly changed underneath.

1986   Sensational motorsport-biased M3 is launched with a special four-cylinder, 238bhp, 2.5-litre twin-cam engine, five-speed transmission, fully reworked chassis and some highly effective aerodynamic aids.

1991   E36 ushered in more flowing styling, better refinement and ergonomics, plus a new multi-link rear suspension to improve handling. Familiar line-up was boosted by a sleek two-door Coupé and the three-door hatchback called 'Compact'. The M3 returned with a new a brawny straight-six 3,201cc engine kicking out 321bhp.

1997   E46 is essentially an evolution of the previous range, chiefly majoring on extended use of aluminium chassis components.

DRIVING

There are minimal complaints here as the 3 Series is one of the most satisfying cars you can drive, either sportingly or in a relaxed mode, and it improved with each generation. The higher-powered E21 and E30 cars need watching in the wet as they can become twitchy – ditto early Compacts. It's generally regarded that the 190bhp/206lb ft 2.8-litre (328) is the ideal all-rounder, but there's an undeniable feel-good factor that comes as standard with any 3 Series.

BUYING TIPS

With so many around, the choice will bamboozle and as a result you should take time in deciding which exact model you want before going shopping. Don't buy the first you see as there's no shortage on sale and their condition varies enormously. Body rust and previous accident repairs should be high on your watching brief. Mechanically, as long as the service schedule was kept up to date, there's no outstanding problems, although head gaskets can fail and the engines burn oil, plus the VANOS valve-timing system fitted to the later six-cylinder engine can play up.

PRICES

Prices are all over the place, starting from under £2,000 for a usable E36, rising to over six figures for an immaculate E30 M3. Condition seems to count more than engine size and body style on E36/E46 and there are loads around for under £4,000. Earlier E21 and E30 models are commanding good money, especially the 323i and the 325i Sport, which can be worth almost double that of a normal E30.

VERDICT

Despite huge popularity the 3 Series is now emerging as a classic. But this isn't the case for all of them, plus there is a lot of dross around. And, as satisfying the 3 Series is, do the sheer numbers around rather negate what many look for in a classic?

BMW 1500, 1800, 2000 & 2002

The BMWs that saved the brand and provided the foundation for the 3 Series. Classy, they are appreciated by those who like BMWs rather than Beemers...

DATES TO REMEMBER

1961 Four-door 1500 saloon; the range is known as 'Neue Klasse'.

1963 1500 replaced by 1800, boosting power from 80bhp to 90bhp.

1964 Rare 110bhp 1800Ti.

1966 1800 up-gunned to 2000 for 100bhp, identified by novel lozenge-shaped headlamps. Smaller, similar-engineered 02 range (02 insignia stood for two-doors) introduced starting with the 1.6-litre 83bhp 1602.

1968 Iconic 2002 launched with 2-litre 100bhp power.

1971 Legendary fuel-injected 2002 Tii introduced packing 130bhp – a few with five-speed transmissions.

1972 Hatchback 2002 Touring joins range, but for UK markets comes only with standard engine; 2000 now replaced by new 5 Series.

1973 Scintillating 170bhp 02 Turbo heads range. Left-hand drive only and luridly emblazoned, this was the forerunner to the M3.

1975 Before 02 bows out to make way for the first 3 Series, an economy 1502 is launched with 75bhp power.

DRIVING

These saloons are worlds away from the finely tuned and refined 3 Series, and as a consequence even seasoned BMW owners stepping back in time may be in for a shock! Although good to drive, they can be tail-happy, especially the higher-powered cars, but overall performance is lively with the Tii models being GTi-quick. Apart from their pep and smoothness, if there is a characteristic common to BMWs of this era it is their inherent low gearing, making cruising slightly fussy.

BUYING TIPS

Despite a first-class owners' club, owning pre-3-Series BMWs isn't as easy as the later Beemers. Parts supply can be patchy and expensive, while rust can run riot. The Kugelfischer fuel-injection system is pretty reliable, just as long as the car is regularly used; long periods of idleness result in problems. Early gearboxes wear, but the later E21 unit also fits and is an accepted upgrade, as are E21 hubs using 5- or 6-Series brake callipers. Steering can feel sloppy but can be adjusted out, and watch for models with twin brake servos as they are dear to fix. Trim is hard-wearing, but you'd be very lucky to find a good original interior.

PRICES

In general, the 1500–2000 saloons are the cheapest buys, starting from around £5,000 although a Tii (never officially marketed in the UK), the rare 1800s with a five-speed gearbox and the UK special-edition, Frazer Nash-BMW badged, 2000ti can command five times as much. The cheapest 02s are the 1502 and the Touring with fairly good cars available from under £7,000, but the 2002s are worth around 25 per cent more and a top Tii will exceed £30,000 with ease.

VERDICT

Made when BMW cars were engineering masterpieces rather than glorified image statements, these early models are for the discerning marque enthusiast who appreciates what the badges really once stood for.

CITROËN DS AND SM

Hailed as the most technically advanced cars of their eras, the charismatic DS and its Maserati-powered coupé SM offshoot attract and demand a special type of enthusiast.

DATES TO REMEMBER

1955   DS saloon launched with radical hyrdropneumatic suspension, steering and braking systems, with semi-auto transmission, all wrapped in a futuristic four-door bodyshell.

1957   A simpler entry model called the ID19 is introduced, lacking hydraulic steering, brakes or gearbox and the interior is more basic. Cars are now built in UK.

1965   New five-bearing engine introduced; 1,985cc or 2,175cc for selective models.

1966/67 Flagship DS21 arrives (1966), an even more radical nose; the major front-end restyle brought twin headlamps for '67.

1969	Fuel-injected version of the DS21 is introduced with 139bhp. All cars gain a revised fascia. 1970 Extrovert-styled SM launched, heavily DS based but with special four-cam Maserati 2.7-litre V6 and a radical coupé body style.
1971	Five-speed transmissions become optional, as do the car's headlamps that turn with the front wheels.
1972	Fuel injection for the SM plus minor chassis tweaks.
1973	Last revamp involving D Supers and the DS23 before DS range is replaced by CX. SM. Gains a larger 3-litre engine and optional automatic transmission.

DRIVING

Not everybody can take to these quirky Citroëns. With a 'button' brake pedal demanding just a light touch, a foot-operated parking brake and hydraulic gear selection, it's like learning to drive all over again. Because of this, you need a long test drive as a quick gallop around the block will have you probably detesting it – made worse on the SM by being LHD only. Common to all are their quite exceptional long-distance cruising abilities thanks to supreme refinement and comfort.

BUYING TIPS

Despite the fact that the DS is 65 years old and the SM more than 50, many are still fearful of the design's complexity and worry about maintenance of the pneumatic system. However, as long as it's properly maintained, it'll remain trouble-free for years, but seek out a good specialist if you don't like home repairs. The DS can rust badly, but so long as the inner skeleton strut is okay, the exterior panels simply bolt on. Structurally, SMs are strong but can suffer suspension stress cracks, which really need a ramp to access properly. The Maserati engine is the main concern and is costly to repair.

PRICES

You can pick up a decent DS for under £5,000, possibly less if you go abroad and buy an LHD version. On the other hand, convertibles sell for crazy money –as much as £150,000! A good DS shouldn't cost much more than £13,000 although a later DS21/23 can command much healthier prices. Realistically, you need to budget for at least £30,000 for a sound SM.

VERDICT

Individual cars for individual people, but you really need a long test drive to see if you can become used to the quirky nature of these Citroëns. Don't let the complexity of their designs put you off, however, as they are very reliable.

CITROËN 2CV AND DERIVATIVES

The 'Tin snail' is more than a basic, cheap and cheerful economy car. It's a practical, characterful classic that also yearns to be used as an everyday runaround hack.

DATES TO REMEMBER

1948	Launched at the Paris Motor Show with 375cc engine (9bhp), known as the 'Tin Snail'.
1961	The Ami offshoot is introduced, identified by Anglia 105E-style reverse-rake rear screen design.
1963	602cc engine now fitted and good for 22bhp plus body receives the now popular 'six window' treatment.
1967/8	Dyane 6 introduced: a 2CV in principle but with a more conventional hatchback body. Range rationalisation: 2CV4 uses new 435cc engine while 2CV6 features a 602cc unit.
1972	Ami receives the larger 1,015cc air-cooled engine inherited from the Citroën GS.
1974	2CV6 relaunched in UK with revised look, updated trim and more, all for £3,000 or so.
1980–82	Charleston has snazzier interior and two-tone exterior paint. Front disc brakes replace drums in '82.
1985	Special Dolly edition is announced, identified by distinctive paintwork.

DRIVING

If you want proof that speed isn't everything, drive a 2CV. A tin snail they truly are, but once wound up they cruise remarkably well in surprising comfort, plus there's no shortage of tuning parts to make them brisker (or for racing purposes), while the Ami Super is an unexpectedly innocuous performer. Handling on all is distinctly roly-poly, but they grip well and again tuning and improving parts are available. Once you get used to the odd dash-mounted gearchange, you'll love the car's quirkiness, but if you want something slightly more conventional, roomier and saner, consider a Dyane. From a practical standpoint, these small Citroëns are masters of versatility – small wonder they are still used as daily drivers.

BUYING TIPS

The good news is that everything you want is available, including new bodies and chassis frames, the latter for around £500. The bad news is that they may well need them as rot is a problem. As the frame twists the steering gets very heavy and lacks self-straightening, clues to watch out for.

Mechanically, they are robust little things. It's usual for the engine to clatter but not excessively so (new engines are around £2,000). Heavy steering can be down to the aforementioned twisted chassis or seized kingpins.

PRICES

Prices vary considerably, from a couple of grand for an average 2CV to perhaps five figures. The best models are post 1976 and, preferably, versions from 1980 because they feature front disc brakes and hydraulic dampers. Before you buy, check out the fully reconditioned and guaranteed 2CVs on sale from specialists, such as 2CV Centre and 2CV City. The best bargains are the Ami and Dyane, costing up to 50 per cent less.

VERDICT

Frugal, friendly, functional, flexible and always fun – is there a better way of telling the world that you're skint than hooning around in a 2CV as your chosen classic? You won't be alone, though, as they enjoy a massive following.

CATERHAM SEVEN

Sevens are heaven for the true enthusiast as they are the closest thing to driving a single-seater on the road, and few classics are as simple and low cost to own.

DATES TO REMEMBER

1957	Launched as the Lotus Mk7.
1961	The Ford power era starts, initially using the Anglia 105E engine in 997cc and 1,340cc formats, the latter used in the larger Classic and Capri.
1970	Squarer-cut S4 takes over with new chassis design.
1973	New owners Caterham revert to old S3 styling and Elan twin-cam engines.
1985–88	De Dion rear suspension option.
1986	HPC 1700 model launched.
1989	'Prisoner' spec special edition released to celebrate the car's apperance in *The Prisoner*.
1990/91	Vauxhall Astra 2-litre 16V engine option, followed by Rover K-Series engine alternative.

1992	Ultimate JPE (Jonathan Palmer Evolution) tops bill with 250bhp Vauxhall power. 35th Anniversary model wears Lotus racing colours.
1998	MGF VVC (150bhp) added to create VVC and VVC Roadsport range. Silver Anniversary Seven revives aluminium body construction– just 30 made.
1999	Fastest ever Seven comes in the shape of the Superlight R500.
2000	Roomier SV boasts a much roomier cockpit and embraces Honda Blackbird superbike power to shattering effect.

DRIVING

A giant go-kart, a super Seven really is the closest thing to a racer on the road, and despite being well over 60 years old, it is still the purest drive you are ever likely to experience. In fact, only the Lotus Elise – 30 years younger – comes close to the experience. Lotus or Caterham, what's best? For hard-core purists with a sense of history or ardent *The Prisoner* fans, that's easy, but in cold clinical terms, the Caterham models are vastly superior in every department.

BUYING TIPS

If you want to strike lucky with a Seven, it's best to gen up on them before your search. There are almost as many varieties as there are cars built – over eighty at the last count. Factory-made cars are usually the most desirable. Accident damage isn't hugely common, but invariably it's frontal impacts where second suspension legs are the most likely areas to be damaged. Rot is not a big concern.

PRICES

Caterhams can be among the cheapest classics you can own, and this includes insurance costs as their accident and theft rates are amazingly low. Given the huge choice of models, you should really enlist the help of a known Caterham specialist, but for the first-time owner, a 1990s Rover-engined K-Series version or the higher-powered Supersports are the best bets. Again, a wide choice means it's hard to pin down prices, but a typical price bracket is usually between £12,000 and £40,000, with the rare and harder-core models valued the most, as are original Lotus variants.

VERDICT

This purest of sports cars has stood the test of time brilliantly, and there's still little to touch these four-wheeled neanderthal classics for raw fun. Just buy one that suits you the best rather than for outright speed.

DAIMLER SP250

(Historics Auctioneers)

Not the best-looking sports cars, it has to be said, but the Daimler SP250's real timeless beauty lies under the skin – as many enthusiasts are now pleasantly discovering.

DATES TO REMEMBER

1959   SP250 launched with a chassis cribbed heavily from the Triumph TR design, powered by the now legendary 2.5-litre 140bhp V8.

1961   Now under Jaguar control, automatic gearbox (but not to superior Police spec) is optional. B-Spec SP250 features a strengthened chassis and revised interior trim. Externally, front and rear bumpers are now fitted.

1963   C-Spec has appointment changes but car's unpopularity and rivalry with Jaguar's E-Type sees the production axed after less than 3,000 made, but not after Jaguar toys with a restyled SP52, which looks remarkably like an Aston Martin DB5 Volante!

DRIVING

Saying that the Daimler drives better than it looks is not a back-handed compliment. That wonderful turbine-like V8 is the SP250's trump card, posting performance as good as a Triumph TR6. Actually the Daimler feels much like a big-engined TR3, although the 2.5-litre, while flexible, does lack torque, which is why automatic suits the car very well. Handling is acceptable so long as the B-Spec improvements are incorporated, but the firm, crashy ride and a lack of refinement for a Daimler surprises, although with an adjustable steering column and good interior space, it's a fine tourer.

BUYING TIPS

Being fibreglass, there's no rust, although the body can craze and crack. The steel chassis rots and so needs a careful check, especially around the suspension and steering. The post-1960 stronger chassis features bracing and stiffening beams. Although known to burn oil (as much as a pint per 600 miles, even when healthy) the V8 can cover 250,000 miles between rebuilds. While the Daimler is closely based on the Triumph TR chassis and transmission, their parts aren't interchangeable. If you want overdrive, a TR gearbox can be adapted to fit, as can a Jaguar Mk2 combo, although this is a harder exercise.

PRICES

After being a cheap classic for many years, SP250s are now hitting the bulls-eye. Really nice SPs sell for £38–£43,000 while the very best examples are £50–£55,000 and a project worth saving starts at £15–£18,000. A-, B- and C-Spec cars are all worth the same; autos are quite desired but don't carry a premium. Ex-police cars are worth more as they enjoy a special 'hold' button for better acceleration. The car's survival rate is pleasingly high so you have a fair opportunity to cherry pick.

VERDICT

A dowdy yet delightful 1950s-styled sports car, the SP250 proves that beauty is only skin deep. The Daimler enjoys a loyal following and the ever-enthusiastic owners' club ensures one is as easy as a Triumph TR to own and run.

FERRARI DINO 246GT

(Historics Auctioneers)

Despite the Dino not being regarded as a true Ferrari, this once entry-level model to the marque has become one of the most loved Ferrari models ever.

DATES TO REMEMBER

1968 Launched in tandem with a Fiat Dino, the first Ferrari was known as the 206GT, featuring an all-aluminium bodywork. The Fiat-built V6 engine also had a capacity of 1,986cc, and while Ferrari claimed more power it was exactly the same engine.

1969 Dino is revised to the much more familiar 246GT sporting a longer wheelbase, clad in a steel body and powered by a larger 195bhp 2.4-litre engine.

1970 So-called Series II cars gained Cromodora alloy wheels plus other improvements.

1971 Series III cars saw revised gearing.

1972 Known in the trade as the 'Flares and chairs' option, it includes better seats and flared wheel arches to accommodate the wider tyres . Also announced this year was the GTS Spider with a lift-out targa top.

DRIVING

The Dino drives almost as divine as it looks. Mid-engined, the handling was considered excellent in its day and still impresses with thanks to its exquisite balance and delicacy if not outright grip. As one road test remarked in 1971, 'When it comes to getting around corners the Ferrari Dino has all the advantages – and makes use of them.' Similarly, the performance is fast but not furious and today a good GTi can outstrip one, not helped by the Ferrari's peak torque being so high in the rev range, meaning you have to use the superb gearbox liberally. Crucially, a Dino makes all the right noises, and its period performance will be enough for the majority of enthusiasts.

BUYING TIPS

If ever a classic has been made better now than when it was new, the Dino must be in the top five as they were very badly made at the factory! One well-known Ferrari specialist once told me that, in his experience, nine out of ten Dinos that he had in his workshops were rubbish before a much-needed restoration was carried out. Rust is ruinously rampant just about everywhere; a professional inspection by a marque expert is essential. The V6 can cost six figures to rebuild and camshaft wear is common.

PRICES

With Dinos you get what you pay for and there are no bargain steals left. Showroom fresh, RHD samples can sell for £450–£500,000 and merely good ones command £350,000, but these figures can only be guides. What is concrete is this advice from Dino experts: it's better to break the bank and buy the best you can from a reputable specialist than go the other route and buy a £150,000 project – because at least it will be correctly restored in the first place.

VERDICT

Dinos are cautious buys and prices are exorbitant, especially considering the car was never officially badged or regarded as a 'real' Prancing Horse. But style-wise, has Ferrari ever bettered the Dino more than half a century on?

FERRARI BB

(Historics Auctioneers)

Ferrari's first mid-engined supercar, the twelve-cylinder BB (short for Berlinetta Boxer) has a hard-earned reputation for being truly tantalising to drive and yet remains a relative bargain.

DATES TO REMEMBER

1973   Originally launched as the 365 GT4 BB to replace the Daytona with a semi-monocoque all-steel frame and a fibreglass floor. The body has a racing-car-like unique clamshell.

1976   Replacing the 365BB was the 512BB (standing for 5 litres and 12 cylinders), identified by a special two-tone paint scheme.

1981   512i signifies Bosch K-Jetronic fuel injection. Only 387 365BBs were made (less than sixty RHD), 929 512BBs (128 UK models) and just over 1,000 BBis, with just under fifty being earmarked for the UK.

DRIVING

The Berlinetta Boxer is an old-school, mid-engined supercar and as such demands respect. Fast in its day, the flat-twelve is always a thrill to use, with many experts regarding the 365 as the nicest of them all. Handling certainly demands attentiveness as it's no delicate Dino, and it can catch out the unwary if pushed too far. Don't fret, though, because unless track driven, most will find the BB brilliant within its limits, and as a cruiser it boasts one of the best Ferrari cabins with a mass of instruments and switchgear to gaze over. For a two-seater space is good, the only black spot being limited rearward visibility due to those heavy buttresses.

BUYING TIPS

Having a Ferrari expert vet a potential buy could save you thousands of pounds and lots of worry. A service history is important as is use, as little-driven BBs are likely to give the most trouble, claim specialists. Rust shouldn't be a major issue as the chassis is sturdy and the engine is as strong as an ox – good thing too, as flat-twelve experts are scarce in the UK. The transmission can be the car's biggest worry, from clutches to differentials, and being Italian, don't expect the electrics to be perfect. Check the tyres: this Ferrari chiefly ran on Michelins, initially XWX before going metric (TRX), but due to their availability and prices, others may be fitted along with modern rubber, which may not suit the BB's chassis.

PRICES

BB could well stand for 'bargain buy' as they are cheaper than equivalent Dino 246GTs and give you a lot more Ferrari for your money at around £300–325,000, although the 1976 ex-Maranello Concessionaires demonstrator and press car, and the first BB in the UK, failed to sell at auction for a bargain £150,000 not so long ago. So have a good look around and study the market before parting with your money.

VERDICT

Even Ferrari experts call them a 'marmite' model but when new in some circles the BB was considered 'Ferrari's greatest supercar yet' and Enzo's answer to the Lamborghini Miura. Enough said.

FERRARI 308-348

(Historics Auctioneers)

Following in the tyre tracks of the delightful Dino was always going to prove tough, but Ferrari not only managed it but also created a better supercar as well as a nailed-on classic.

DATES TO REMEMBER

1975   Replacement for the lukewarm 2+2 GT4 really was the spiritual successor to the Dino as the basic platform was employed. The first 712 cars are clothed in a glass-fibre body and were built by Scaglietti.

1977   A 300lb-heavier steel body takes over and as a result, the earlier cars quickly became highly collectible. The same year, a targa-topped GTS, similar to the Dino 246, is introduced.

1981   Power-sapping emission-friendly fuel injection is fitted, dropping power to 214bhp as a result.

1982   New four-valve cylinder head returns power up to 240bhp. Now badged as the 308 QV (*quattrovalvole*) the build quality improves and better rust protection is also employed.

1985   A thoroughly facelifted 328 replaces the 308, plus there's now a larger 3,185cc V8.

1989   348 supersedes the 328 (after 7,412 examples of the latter have been built) with bulkier Testarossa look. Changes underneath include a 3.4-litre engine upgrade, now mounted north–south, allied to a transverse-mounted transmission.

1990   Substantial chassis rethink to cure nervous handling as power is raised to 320bhp and
        model renamed simply as GTB and GTS.

DRIVING

Of this trio, the 308 and 328 are the most rewarding drives as even a hurried suspension reset on
the 348 never truly endeared it to Ferrari fans, despite its added grunt, whereas the earlier cars
had a Dino flavour about them. The lighter, plastic-fantastic 308s are the best, being more agile,
although if you've never sampled one, you won't appreciate such differences.

BUYING TIPS

As with all supercars, Ferraris need proper inspections by experts, so if you don't know what
you're looking for, then enlist the help of one. Failing this, the owners' club will help (ferrariown-
ersclub.co.uk). Unless you want a specific car, don't be choosy over colour or model; condition and
a strong service history are what really count. The tubular-steel structure can corrode as can the
bulkheads. There was no galvanising until 1982, but all 328s were fully protected. Mechanically,
the design is tough if well serviced and used regularly.

PRICES

The 348 is the cheapest and a fair car can be yours for £50,000 or so, which is half the price of
a comparable 308 or 328, with the plastic 308 'Vetroresinas' worth as much as £150,000. But
whether it's a 308 or a 328, it's the mandatory red with cream hide interior that everybody wants
with a 308, although some experts reckon the 328 is far more usable and better built.

VERDICT

Cheer if you can't afford a Dino 246GT, as this fantastic threesome make for a more usable and
far more affordable Ferrari. They are also the more durable although you still need to take extra
care when buying one.

FIAT 500

(Author)

Another economy car that wormed its way into the hearts of its owners and became a cult classic, the Fiat 500 is still a sensible, usable and inexpensive-to-run second car.

DATES TO REMEMBER

1957   The 500 is launched, debuting Fiat's first air-cooled, twin-cylinder engine – a 13bhp, 479cc unit – but it is quickly retuned to give 15bhp before production begins. Novel features include a roll-back fabric sunroof (to save precious metal) and suicide doors. There are two models: Economy and Standard.

1958   500 Sport joins range with 21.5bhp.

1960   A full 500cc liberates 17.5bhp and the family-friendly 500 estate debuts badged Giardiniera, which survives until 1977.

1965   The 500F debuts, featuring conventional front doors, a larger windscreen and a slight power increase: 18bhp!

1968   Lusso (500L) ushers in added trim, radial tyres and even a proper fuel gauge.

1972   Final 500 is the 500R, using the same 23bhp, 594cc engine fitted to the new 126. Production ceases three years later, after nearly 3.5 million saloons and over 320,000 Giardinieras have been made.

DRIVING

Despite their lack of power, smiles per miles are always guaranteed with any 500 thanks to their nimble handling and light, precise controls. Add the mighty mouse's diminutive size, allowing the Fiat to squeeze into tiny gaps, and it still makes a great city commuter car. If you want more power, there's no shortage of tuning parts to make one pleasingly zippy, although just the fitment of the later and cheaper 126 engine easily suffices. Don't overlook the bigger 600, which enjoys the same *joie de vivre* but with more room and performance; discontinued by 1970.

BUYING TIPS

In our climate, 500s rust just about everywhere and especially at the stern, but at least panel supply is good (less so detailed trim bits), although whether a full restoration is economically viable is questionable. Engines are inherently noisy and if the dipstick is being ejected from its aperture, it is probably because the crankcase is becoming pressurised due to wear, plus the air-cooled unit is prone to overheating and leaking oil. Gearboxes can be weak, but again the 126 comes to the rescue here.

PRICES

Prices vary enormously with projects starting from around £2,000, ranging to concours-crafted cars that can cost ten times this. Reasonably good cars command at least £10,000 with the 600 being appreciably cheaper, save for the innovative mini MPV Multipla, which can achieve between £15,000 and £30,000. Sporting Abarths sell for equally crazy money – as much as £60,000 – with the rarer Austrian-built Styer-Puch alternatives equally as fast, and expensive.

VERDICT

The 500 is an endearing little thing that, like Citroën's 2CV, also doubles up as fun second car. Buy well and you'll have a car that's easy to work on, cheap to fix and restore (if it needs it) and lots of fun to have around.

FIAT DINO

(Historics Auctioneers)

A Dino by another name and also built at Maranello, but the Fiat version is, in its own way, just as desirable and, of course, so much cheaper. And dare we say, the rarer classic?

DATES TO REMEMBER

1966   Fiat's Dino launched to replace the Fiat 2300S around the same time as the Ferrari, which shared the same engine. Spider and coupé look so different, as dropheads were styled and built by Pininfarina, while Bertone was responsible for the fixed-heads.

1969   Most significant revamp. In common with the Ferrari, the engine is stretched to 2.4 litres (the engine's block being iron) and the rear suspension is revised. Minor changes are also made to the styling, and this was pretty much it until the car bowed out in 1972 to make way for the new 130 Coupé after fewer than 1,600 Spiders were made against 7,655 Coupés.

DRIVING

Be in no doubt that this Fiat is no Ferrari in disguise, but it is no less appealing. This Dino has two different characters: the stubbier drophead is by far the sportier pseudo Ferrari, the larger coupé being a refined high-style GT made for touring as depicted in *The Italian Job*, not least because it's a fuller-sized fastback. Performance on both, by today's standards, is barely any better than a modern family car, although with that lovely Dino V6 soundtrack, who cares? Secure handling, care of the new Fiat 130-derived suspension, is superior to the earlier 2300S-sourced leaf-spring set-up, but the Fiat's left-hand-drive format will not suit everybody.

BUYING TIPS

The Fiat badge ensures slightly easier running costs, but that four-cam Dino engine costs £10k to overhaul, whatever the badge. Camshaft wear (more than £1,200 each) is very common to all and the 2.4 is more prone to break its valves, while those triple Weber 40 DCN carbs are pricey to expertly repair and set up. A fair number of mechanical parts came from the humble Fiat 125 and 130 saloons, and so are cheap if hard to find. Rust will naturally be a major issue, with Spiders suffering the worst, and panel availability isn't good. As the Fiat is valued less than the Ferrari, cost up a 'bargain' project with care.

PRICES

Although vastly cheaper than the Ferrari namesake, the Fiats have shot up of late, which means a cool £120,000 or more for the specialist-build Spiders. Coupés remain easy meat at £35–£45,000+ for a good-to-excellent car. As all are left-hand drive, you may strike a better deal by looking abroad; the Germans and Swiss appear to have the best of what's left.

VERDICT

A wonderful and, until recently, vastly underrated affordable supercar, mainly because it wears a Fiat rather than a Ferrari badge. So is this Dino a poor man's Ferrari or a rich man's Fiat? Let the debate begin ...

FIAT X1/9

A baby Ferrari in all but name, Fiat's delightful mid-engined X1/9 bristles with supercar thinking and the seat-of-the-pants finesse you'd expect from a Prancing Horse. And all for the price of a Triumph Spitfire.

DATES TO REMEMBER

1972   Announced in Europe; based upon the Fiat 128 1300 Rally saloon but mid-engined with a novel targa top, styled by Bertone. Other notables include all-independent MacPherson strut suspension and disc brakes all round.

1974   Fiat specialist Radbourne starts to market cars imported into the UK but converted to RHD. The cars were good but too expensive.

1977   Official imports commence at £3,000 but spec includes tinted glass, alloy wheels and specially tailored luggage bags.

1978   Special edition Lido joins range to sign off the original before making way for the revised X1/9, which is identified by bulkier bumpers and higher engine cowl, hiding the new 85bhp 1.5-litre engine and five-speed gearbox taken from the Strada.

1981   Seemingly losing interest in this little gem, Fiat hands the entire production over to Bertone and cars are badged as such from now on.

1982   VS model introduced with a high spec (power windows, leather trim) and is instantly identified by two-tone paintwork and new-style alloy wheels.

1989   Final X1/9 is aptly called the Finale, easily spotted by its blue or red metallic paint, Alcantara trim and an ungainly rear spoiler.

DRIVING

The baby Ferrari boast is fully justified. The X1/9 was way ahead of its time and MG only caught up with its MGF 20 years later. Although frisky rather than thunderous, the Fiat is a joy thanks to its exquisite chassis that responds to a precise fingertip driving style as befitting its mini supercar tag – complete with a cockpit to match. One magazine reckoned 'the Fiat is a smaller, slower cheaper Ferrari' and that sums up the X1/9 quite brilliantly.

BUYING TIPS

Buy with care. Although strong and well constructed, rust is rampant just about everywhere you can think of, and panel supply dried up years ago. The engines are long-lasting with just usual wear points, although they are prone to overheating. This can lead to head-gasket failure due to clogged radiators and coolant pipes. The clutch actuating mechanisms seize although the transmissions are strong. The rear suspension ball joints are unavailable and have to be professionally rebuilt. This is the same for the rear brake callipers, which are unique to the car but at least are available, albeit at £150 a side. The trim doesn't wear too well so expect general tattiness.

PRICES

Starting from the bottom, a project can be had from £500, with usable roadworthy cars from £2,500, but double this for something that catches the eye. Really nice X1/9s sell for £5–£7,500, with showroom specimens going all the way to £10,000 (especially the special edition variants). The much rarer 1.3s command the most.

VERDICT

A brilliant little sports car that fully deserves its baby Ferrari reputation and is the far more sophisticated alternative to a Triumph Spitfire or MG Midget. But you have to buy with care and make allowances for patchy parts supply.

FIAT COUPÉ

Perhaps not the cutest-looking Latin classic but the Italian's brilliant driving manners and value for money more than compensate for any vanity issues.

DATES TO REMEMBER

1993   New Fiat Coupé, based upon the Tipo hatchback platform, debuts in Europe with a 1,995cc 16V engine, in 137bhp normally aspirated or 195bhp turbocharged forms.

1995   Imports start to reach UK dealerships.

1998   A limited edition model, with a run of only of 300 in the UK, debuts.

1999   Major mechanical changes: the 147bhp normally aspirated 20v engine is replaced by a 154bhp 20v VIS (Variable Inlet System) unit with a fly-by-wire throttle, while a six-speed gearbox is now standard. Top is the Turbo Plus sporting a special Viscodrive limited-slip differential, unique 16in wheels and leather trim.

DRIVING

Those in the know will tell you that the ability-rich Fiat Coupé is a better sporting fastback than the more upmarket, yet also Tipo derived, Alfa GTV that was launched around the same time. This is because the Fiat handles so much better, so much so that the Coupé, along with the VW Corrado, were ranked as the best-handling front-wheel-drive cars of their generation. And these Fiats are staggeringly fast, with the 217bhp Integrale five-pot engine well harnessed thanks to its Viscodrive differential. For a coupé the Fiat is surprisingly spacious and the interior boasts some lovely retro touches such as a body-coloured metal dashboard.

BUYING TIPS

The problem is finding a good one out of the comparatively few left. Leading Coupé experts, Solo Italia, add that their lowly values foster neglect and skipped servicing, but thankfully, unlike previous Fiats, it's not a major ruster thanks to good rustproofing. All engines are durable if they are serviced right and have their camshaft and auxiliary belts changed on time, although the actual camshafts wear out. Particular to Turbos are cracking exhaust manifolds and failing turbo units – as the normal engines are brisk enough, do you want a troublesome Turbo where the transmissions will have also had a tougher time? The rest of the oily bits are subject to normal wear and tear. A small but vital point: try to obtain all the keys; from late 1996 there were three of them. The silver one is for everyday use, the blue is the spare, and the red is the one you don't lose at all costs as it's the master key.

PRICES

Prices vary wildly although even the best Turbo Pluses are unlikely to break into five figures, with average-to-good ones hovering around the £5,000 mark. The best value lies in the normally aspirated versions, which aren't slow and in five-cylinder form have all the performance that you're likely to need, and have probably not been driven so hard. The most sought-after Coupés are the Limited Edition (the spec of which became the norm from August 1999), while the Turbo Plus is all about cosmetics as it's mechanically identical.

VERDICT

This Fiat is one of the best modern classics on the block and, when you consider what Lancia Integrales sell for, is a performance bargain – if you can find a good one which hasn't been thrashed to death, that is.

FORD PILOT

(Historics Auctioneers)

Ford's first ever car to be built at Dagenham, if you desire post-war Americana with a British background, the V8-powered Pilot is in a class of its own.

DATES TO REMEMBER

1947   Launched as a saloon and 'woody' estate (a pick-up was also made for export only) with a UK-developed 85bhp, 3,622cc side-valve V8 (based upon the 1937 Model 78 engine), three-speed transmission, 6-volt electrics and part hydraulic brakes. Leather or cloth trim was standard and the front windscreen hinged for added ventilation. A built-in jacking system (Jackall) was also fitted along with a heater (a rare thing back then), carpets, Windtone horns and even a cigarette lighter and steering-column anti-theft lock. The car cost just under £750 at launch in black, light green, dark blue or beige.

DRIVING

Although a V8, the pilot of a Pilot is unlikely to take on a Sierra Cosworth, though in its day the 85bhp provided highly respectable performance. The 0–60 stroll of 20 seconds doesn't tell the whole story thanks to a healthy 140lb ft of torque produced at just 1,500rpm, and the Pilot feels lively away from motorways. The three-speed gearbox means that second acts like a semi-auto and is really responsive from walking pace. Pilots are not for high flyers but, for what they were designed for, handle acceptably – good enough to win the 1950 Tulip Rally, in fact! Ride comfort isn't bad and this old timer has the ability to waft along like a Ford Granada.

BUYING TIPS

For such an oldie, parts supply is generally very good and most of what you need is out there, the exceptions being chrome and detailed trim work. Contact The Early Ford V8 Club of America UK and Ford experts Barry Smith (barrysimthcars.co.uk) for the best advice and assistance.

    The famous flathead is a legend but has its faults, chiefly overheating. It's a simple side-valve engine but still expensive to overhaul (£5,000+) as the crankshaft and heads (the latter aren't unknown to warp) require specialist attention. Transmissions can be a problem and parts are more prevalent in the US.

PRICES

It's estimated that 400–500 survive in various states of fitness. Saloons are the most plentiful with Woodys next. Ute and pick-up versions are like hens' teeth over here, but you'll have better luck in Australasia and South Africa. The closer to standard spec the better, but due to the unavailability of certain trim parts, that's becoming increasingly difficult to achieve. Presentable Pilots can be seen for around £6,000 or so but will need a fair bit of work to make good, and this can be expensive so reckon on three times this for a concours model. Woodies are worth a far bit more and easily break the £20,000 barrier.

VERDICT

A great choice for those seeking a (pseudo) post-war American classic, which is easy to run thanks to good club support and is great fun to own. Easy speed from that tuneable flathead engine comes from variety of US specialists.

FORD ANGLIA AND CLASSIC

(Author)

With its Ford Thunderbird rear fins and that novel reverse-rake rear windscreen, these stylish saloons give classic old-school Ford fans 1950s style.

DATES TO REMEMBER

1959   Anglia 105E launched to replace 100E range with four-cylinder 997cc engine and four-speed gearbox. Mechanically similar but radically styled, with a reserve-rake rear screen.

1961   Estate added to line up along with commercial van. Consul Classic two- and four-door saloon and two-door coupé introduced, essentially similar to Anglia mechanically and in style except for Capri with a 1,340cc engine.

1962   1,200cc engine option for Anglia specifically for upmarket Super trim, with bigger brakes. Larger, more reliable 1,498cc engine for the Consul Classic.

1963   Capri 1500GT announced, forerunner to the Cortina GT, before both ranges are culled.

1965   Detail changes include revised controls with coloured front indicator lights and the optional metallic paint on Supers.

DRIVING

The Anglia was a formidable racer in its day, though the road car isn't so precise and performance is pedestrian, but it is more comfortable and roomier than a Mini. However, as this Ford was so popular with tuners in its day, it still remains a boy racer's delight, resulting in the majority of remaining cars being uprated in some form or other. Bear in mind, though, that Anglias are much sloppier and old fashioned compared to the Escort that displaced it. The Classic and Capri drive much the same but are heavier and stodgier, but all boast front disc brakes. The Classic GT was a real goer in its day.

BUYING TIPS

Being an old-school rear-wheel-drive Ford, DIY couldn't be easier. Parts supply is still pretty good, plus there's a huge mix-and-match interchangeability with other Fords. The biggest fear is rust, as you'd expect, but replacement repair panels are becoming prevalent. Steering-wheel wobble at speed is a characteristic that is difficult to eradicate without replacing everything that's remotely worn. Many Anglias are tuned, and if done well, make especially good buys.

PRICES

Anglias have risen steadily in value, and the thick end of £9,000 is not unknown for a factory-fresh car. Unless it's a period-tuned model, from the likes of Broadspeed or Superspeed, an uprated Anglia shouldn't cost a great deal more than a standard car, although it may well be more desirable. Classics are priced slightly above Anglia prices and Capri GT values are positively soaring – up to £14,000 if concours.

VERDICT

Anglias (and Classic/Capris) are simple, stylish cars providing low-cost motoring, a recipe that appeals to many enthusiasts today just as it did back in 1959. Younger drivers will find this 1960s Ford distinctly cool, too.

FORD ESCORT

(MagicCarPics)

Humble, honest-to-goodness family classic, an enthusiast's delight and motorsport legend, there's an Escort for everybody, but prices are soaring.

DATES TO REMEMBER

1967   Escort replaces Anglia with a full range from base 1100 to the Lotus-powered Twin Cam.

1968   1300GT, based upon the plusher Super, is added to the range featuring a downsized Cortina 1600GT unit for a peppy 72bhp.

1970   RS1600 supersedes Twin Cam (which survived for another year) based on the new Type 49 shell, with a detuned Formula 2 1.6-litre, 120bhp, 16-valve racing engine. Later that year, the Mexico slotted in between the 1300GT and RS. Essentially it's the RS1600 fitted with the normal 86bhp Cortina 1600GT engine.

1971   Rare 1300 Sport features a part-time Type 49 shell and the basic 1100 interior.

1973   Luxury Sport offshoot is the 1300E with the RS2000 utilising the 100bhp Cortina 2000 GXL engine.

1975   Mk2 is based upon the Mk1 platform but with squarer styling. 1300/1600 Sports replaced Mexico, and the RS1600 became the RS1800, but all sporting Escorts are now built on conventional production lines after the closure of the Advanced Vehicles Operation.

1976   New RS Mexico and RS2000.

1979   Special edition Harrier is a restyled 1.6 Sport, while a Sport-powered yet anonymous-looking 1600 L/GL was also on the price lists.

DRIVING

Few classics are better to drive with verve than a well-sorted Escort. The real fun starts with the Mk1 Mexico, with the RS2000 the best all-rounder, more so the excellent Mk2 variant. The droop-snooted Mk2 RS2000 was so well received that it rather made the more exotic and harder to maintain RS1800 superfluous. At the other end of the performance spectrum, the 1300GT and Sports are plucky performers.

BUYING TIPS

Apart from rust, the biggest worry has to be fake RS models, some so convincing that you'd need a Ford expert to verify. Check VIN numbers with the clubs (avoclub.com, rsownersclub.co.uk and seoc.co.uk) to be sure. AVO Mk1s start with BF18 numbers, Mk2 Mexicos and RS2000s carry a GCAT number, RS1800 a BBAT or GCAT and added GTAR code. Genuine AVO parts are thin on the ground although admittedly panel supply is good.

PRICES

All Escorts have shot up in value to the point even mainstream 1300L rep's cars and vans fetch £10,000. GTs and RS alternatives can achieve up to five times this depending on model and provenance. Twin Cams and RS1600s lead the charge followed by Mk2 RS2000s, although the rarity of the Mk2 Mexico alternative is starting to pay dividends.

VERDICT

Escorts are blue-collar classics that fit in just about anywhere. The sportier models are great down-to-earth fun cars, which enjoy a firm following and their increasing value ensures they appeal to the head as well as the heart.

FORD CORTINA AND CORSAIR

(Author)

The Cortina is one of those cars that most of us remember for various reasons. Plain and simple, they are enormous fun and, best of all, you don't have to buy a Lotus to enjoy one.

DATES TO REMEMBER

1962   Cortina announced, replacing the Consul Classic and utilising Anglia 1200 hardware in two- and four-door styles.

1963   1.5-litre 83bhp GT and 105bhp Lotus performance versions added to range with new 1,498cc option on mainstream models. More upmarket Corsair 1500/GT introduced on roomier floorpan and American Thunderbird-like styling.

1966   Mk2 replacement has more angular lines.

1967   Iconic 1600E tops range alongside new Cortina-Lotus Mk2 (rebadged Twin-Cam) and 2000E Corsair.

1970   All-new Mk3 Cortina replaces old Cortina and Corsair ranges with overhead-cam (OHC) 1600 GT/2000 'Pinto' engine options.

1976 Mk4 is essentially a rebody on the old floorpan with updated trim options. GT replaced by S versions.

1979 Cortina 80 (unofficially better known as Mk5) is sharper looking facelift. Sports S pack option replaces old range.

DRIVING

There are two types, pre and post Mk3s, and they possess entirely different personalities, with the former the more austere and active, the latter being more palatial and better for cruising. Best are the GTs and better still the legendary 1600E, the latter care of its excellent interior and Lotus suspension. Early Mk3s were roly-poly handlers, although they were much improved for 1974. The Mk4/Mk5 have shades of the Mk2 about them and are the better drivers, especially with the optional S suspension. The larger Corsair drives much like a Cortina albeit with more refinement and is not a bad performer in top 2000E tune.

BUYING TIPS

With the newest Cortina nearly 40 years old, endemic rust is rife on all cars so expect to see rot or past repairs. Panel supply isn't bad but it depends on the model and the panel required – Corsairs fare the worst not unexpectedly. Being a Ford, parts are no problem, new or used, and of course there's tremendous interchangeability across the ranges as well as the chance to update.

PRICES

The TV series *Life on Mars* had a significant impact on Mk3 values and these are some of the priciest, along with their predecessors. The best Mk3s can see price tags of around £7,000 with the Mk1/Mk2 trailing by not much, and £5,000 should buy a good Cortina of any year, the exception being the 1600E which can realise double this. Aside from the Mk4 and Cortina 80 series, the best bargains are the Corsairs. Most of the surviving Mk2s are 1600Es and Lotuses, meaning De Luxes and Supers are now thin on the ground, and of those that are left few are in really good condition, which now means any exceptional ones can command very good prices.

VERDICT

Cortina was a landmark Ford and one of the cars that defined the 1960s. There's still a copious number around, although Mk1s and Mk2s are the rarest. The sports models are best, but don't overlook a good Corsair.

FORD CAPRI

(Historics Auctioneers)

The car 'you always promised yourself' is still one that's well worth pursuing as there's a 'British Mustang' for most budgets and tastes, and they are rapidly increasing in value.

DATES TO REMEMBER

1969 Capri coupé re-introduced, now broadly based upon a mix of Escort and Cortina Mk2 components with 1.3–2.0-litre (V4) engines and three trim packs: X, L and R.

1970 Zodiac-powered 128bhp V6 joins range; 3000E is the top model.

1971 Improvements across the range, most newsworthy being the uprated V6 liberating an added 10bhp.

1972 Over 150 changes, including major suspension tweaks and a new interior are part of the summer revise with the 3000E now replaced by the GXL.

1973 RS3100 is a motorsport special with Group 2 racing in mind; 248 were officially built.

1974 Three-door hatchback Capri II is based on original platform with Ghia now being the top trim option, and the old 2-litre V4 is replaced by Escort RS2000 power.

1978 Mk3 is identified by new front styling but there are few mechanical changes.

1981 3-litre Essex engine is replaced by new Granada EFI engine and a retuned chassis to create the 2.8i.

1982 Special Tickford Capri unveiled with a turbocharged 205bhp 2.8-litre engine with fully revised chassis and brakes.

DRIVING

Although intrinsically Cortina-based, the Capri has a character of its own and is far more pleasurable to drive with crisper handling due to more precise rack-and-pinion steering taken from the Escort, although brakes were always a weak spot. Predictably, it's the GT and V6 versions that hold the most appeal, the latter enjoying a mini muscle car disposition, although they can be tail happy in the wet. Four-cylinder variants are also fun with the 2-litre the best. Capri 2s have a softer nature, although power steering became a welcome option on the V6s. Capri 3s feel the most stable at speed, and five-speed transmissions were provided on late cars.

BUYING TIPS

Erosion attacks everywhere, but quality aftermarket panels are available from Ex-Press Steel and Magnum. Excellent mechanical interchangeability with the Cortina and Escort makes parts availability easy. A proper factory V6 Capri is much better to drive than any conversion, not least because the bodyshell was specially strengthened, plus the transmission, suspension, steering geometry and brakes were also uprated to suit. There are no real surprises mechanically although certain V4 and V6 components (both of which can strip their timing gear or snap their oil pump drive shafts) are becoming scarce and the characteristic steering shimmy can prove very difficult to eradicate.

PRICES

Values have soared and there are few bargains, although the surprisingly unpopular Capri 2 is usually the cheapest of the triad. Mk1s can sell for £25,000 if a vivacious V6, and double this for RS3100s. If you want something cheaper, a 2.8i is the answer and a decent one can be had for £10,000, with the exception of a Brooklands 280. For those with less than £5,000 to spend then a Capri 2 is the safest buy.

VERDICT

An uncomplicated stylish 1970s classic that's easy to own yet always turn heads, a good many owners are buying them once again for old times' sake. Capris are so much more than a Cortina in prettier clothing!

FORD CONSUL, ZEPHYR AND ZODIAC

(Author)

If ever a British classic shouts Rock and Roll, it's Ford's Zephyr and Zodiac, a car that epitomised that glamorous golden era of fins and things motoring. If you want a classic to cruise in, few do it better and none are as easy to own.

DATES TO REMEMBER

1950   EOTTA was the name for all-new 1,508cc Consul, the first unitary-construction Ford, which also ushered in the MacPherson Strut suspension design.

1951   Upmarket Zephyr with choice of four- and six-cylinder engine options, identified by different grille treatment. Convertible range also announced.

1953   Flagship six-cylinder Zodiac announced with better trim and slightly more power.

1956   Mk2 ranges announced with more flowing lines, bigger 1,703cc and 2,553cc engines.

1962   Mk3 Zephyr 4, Zephyr 6 and Zodiac introduced but Consul line-up is dropped in favour of the Zephyr 4 range.

1965   Zodiac Executive tops range, but overdrive option is now no longer available on Zephyr 4.

1966   All new square-cut MkIV Zephyr and Zodiac replaces Mk3s boasting (2-litre) V4 and (2.5- and 3.0-litre) V6 engines, independent rear suspension and all-round disc brakes. Executive has a steel sunroof.

DRIVING

All models are at their best when cruising along, letting the Ford's brawny straight-six engines do their work in top gear. Handling is typically wishy-washy but as good as any, unlike the MkIV replacement which was roundly criticised not only for its wallow-prone ways and ludicrously low-geared steering (as many as six turns lock-to-lock), but also its skittish tail. Wider modern radial tyres help enormously. As you'd expect, Consuls and Zephyr 4s are appreciably slower.

BUYING TIPS

A Ford badge will always ensure the easiest of running, but parts for these big Fords aren't as widespread as for the company's more popular classics. Saying that, most of what you need is available if you search hard enough. As conventional as classics can be, all models are a DIYer's delight, with the exception of the rear disc brakes on the MkIV which require special tools. Apart from the usual rot spots – which are pretty much everywhere – on the Mk3, the heater box air intake rots and weakens the bulkhead. Being less stressed, the six-cylinder engines are the most reliable runners. Certain V engine parts are becoming scarce and these units are prone to stripping their timing cogs and shearing the drive to the oil pump.

PRICES

All things being equal, the pre-Mk3 ranges set the higher prices, and top Zephyrs and Zodiacs are worth well over £10,000 and perhaps as much as £15,000, with convertibles adding at least 50 per cent to the bill. Good examples will achieve just over £7,000 for a saloon. Zodiacs are usually priced a bit more than a Zephyr 6 although condition counts the most. The best bargains are the MkIVs, although for how much longer is questionable as values are creeping up. As it now stands, a good MkIV realises under £4,000.

VERDICT

If you can't quite stretch to a good Jaguar Mk1 or Mk2, why not look to these Fords as a viable alternative? And don't turn your nose up at a lower-powered Consul either, if speed isn't a priority, or a good MkIV.

FAST FORDS

(Histories Auctioneers)

Successor to the fabled RS line, the XR for the 1980s and '90s gives the same thrills under a different badge yet still retains what people love most about fast Fords – their 24/7 usability.

DATES TO REMEMBER

1980 First XR is the Escort XR3, with its all new CVH 94bhp 1.6-litre powerplant.

1981 XR2 is the feistiest Fiesta yet with a Mk2 Cortina 1600GT-derived engine and retuned chassis developed by Ford's SVE division.

1983 Five-speed transmissions for XR3, plus engine uprated to fuel injection for 108bhp. Motorsport-orientated 115bhp RS1600i is a special XR3i, albeit with unique engine and chassis tweaks. Sierra XR4i has Capri 2.8i engine and is identified by novel bi-plane rear wings fitted to the three-door body.

1984 New XR2 utilises old XR3 engine.

1985 Escort RS Turbo has potent 132bhp turbocharged engine. Motorsport-biased RS Sierra Cosworth packs special 200bhp in a big-winged three-door bodyshell.

1988 Less flamboyant Sierra Cosworth inherits four-door Sapphire body.

1990 New XR2i with fuel injection launched, Cosworth Sierra gains all-wheel drive.

1991 New Escort range sees a 128bhp, 1.8-litre (Zetec), 16-valve XR3i launched along with a 150bhp RS2000; (Granada) Scorpio 24V has special Cosworth-tuned 2.8 V6 allied to automatic transmission and luxury trim.

1992 Sierra Cosworth morphs into the Escort Cosworth. Two highly potent Fiestas head range; 128bhp RS1800i and 132bhp RS Turbo.

1993 RS2000 4x4 uses Cosworth chassis with the milder 150bhp engine and less assertive styling.

2001 RS Focus launched with 212bhp 2-litre turbocharged Duratec engine.

DRIVING

One can only generalise but all provide that unique fast Ford feel – scintillating classics such as the Sierra Cosworth heroically so. Standout models include all Sierra and Escort RS Cosworths, the vastly underrated RS2000 (especially the 4x4), the sweet-performing RS1800i Fiesta, the RS Focus and the back-to-basics original XR2 and XR3.

BUYING TIPS

Rust together with previous and possibly badly repaired accident damage are the biggest worries, particularly on RS models to which you can also add fakes and theft. By nature, all fast Fords will have been driven hard.

PRICES

There's fast Ford for everybody, starting from less than £3,000 in the case of the surprisingly satisfying Scorpio 24V to £50,000 and above for concours RS-badged Fords, with three-door Sierras and Escorts topping the list. Frisky Focuses in good condition are currently valued at £10,000 and you may be able to get hold of a very tidy early XR2 and XR3 for a similar amount. The RS2000 and the RS1800i, the latter costing £7,000 which can be half the price of an RS Turbo, are the best bargains along with the Focus.

VERDICT

Their soaring popularity means prices can only go one way and you need to search out the sound, unmolested examples as well as being prepared to wait for the right fast Ford to turn up. It will be worth it.

FORD MUSTANG

(Author)

A legendary product of marketing slickness, Mustang promised ordinary motorists a taste of the good life and are as easy to drive and own as our Capri.

DATES TO REMEMBER

1964   Mustang in coupé and convertible guises is launched, based upon the Falcon floorpan with a choice of trims, options and six-cylinder and V8 engines.

1965   Fastback added to line-up along with legendary Shelby performance models.

1967   Now using the Fairlane platform, Shelby Cobra range is topped by awesome 355bhp, 428ci GT500.

1968   Shelby's GT500KR, standing for 'King of the Road', introduced, while 7-litre 390bhp joins normal range.

1973	Mustang 2 is smaller and more economy biased with Pinto four-cylinder power.
1975–77	Return of the V8 and Cobra 2 plus T-top option.
1979	Mustang 3 is underpinned by new Fox-chassis.
1982	5-litre V8 Mustang GT goes on sale.
1984	SVO performance line-up introduced.
1994	Fox 4 (S-95) replacement ushers in new engines, and facelifted in '96.
2005	Mk4 (S195) sees return of original Mustang style combined with new engines and front suspension. Mk6 (S550) followed in 2015.

DRIVING

Without wishing to pour cold water on this icon, by and large Mustangs don't drive particularly sportily. Yes, the V8s have power to spare, but the handling, especially on pre-Fox models, is not unlike the Capri but softer. The Fox chassis improved things considerably so the later the car the better, but as a driver's car real strides only came with the Mk5. Almost 75 per cent of Mustangs were initially V8 powered and automatic, and a lot more have been retro converted, but there's little wrong with the others if all you want to do is cruise. Ford marketed RHD cars for a couple of years.

BUYING TIPS

It's no exaggeration to say a Mustang is as easy to keep as a Capri or an MGB. Parts supply is an industry in itself and anything from a widget to a new body is available for the Mk1. The others are also well looked after and this goes for a massive range of tuning and improving components. Check out the Mustang Owners' Club of Great Britain (www.mocgb.net). Rust can be terminal on all Mustangs, although less of a worry on Fox-bodied cars.

PRICES

There's a Mustang for every budget. At the top end, the Mk1 rules the roost, as even remotely sound cars command the thick end of £20,000. Fastbacks and convertibles command 50 per cent more; Shelbys at least £100,000, but double this for the best genuine cars. In contrast, the Mustang 2 is by far the cheapest prospect as a few thousand will buy something trustworthy, but values are rising for the nicest ones, especially the long-underrated Cobras. The S95 range are regular £6,000 buys with Mk5s priced a bit more but still sit comfortably under £10,000, depending on trim, etc.

VERDICT

Even those who aren't fans of American cars generally make exceptions for the Mustang because they look and feel kind of 'European'. My choice, apart from the original variants naturally, is the Mk5 for its retro styling.

JAGUAR XK120/140

(Author)

Jaguar's first grand tourer has 1950s class and style to spare, and may well finally stop you longing for that E-Type that you always dreamed about.

DATES TO REMEMBER

1948   XK120 is initially a roadster made from aluminium and featuring the all-new 3,442cc twin-cam straight-six XK engine.

1950   After 242 aluminium cars, steel production takes over.

1951   Fixed-Head Coupé (FHC) added to range, plus a Special Equipment (SE) option for more power (from 160bhp to 180bhp) harnessed by stiffer torsion bars and uprated rear leaf suspension springs.

1953   Drophead Coupé receives winding windows and a heavily lined hood.

1954   XK140 is an evolution of XK120 with a longer body for 2+2 seating and more cabin space. SE (1955) is boosted to 210bhp thanks to the fitment of a C-type cylinder head. Overdrive is now optional and there's also rack-and-pinion steering.

1957   XK150 supersedes XK140 and is identified by a single-piece windscreen; 190bhp for the regular model and 250bhp in S form with disc brakes all round.

1959   3,781cc boosts power to 220bhp, uprated S offers 265bhp.

DRIVING

All feel distinctly old-fashioned when compared to the E-Type, although highly enjoyable nevertheless. The XK120 is the most dated to drive, and most enthusiasts will feel happier with the later cars, which are not unlike a two-seater Mk1 saloon. Brakes, steering and ride are from another era, but for all that, a well-sorted and adjusted XK feels very sprightly, more so when accepted mods and upgrades, including front disc brakes, are dialled in. In fact, many XKs have been modernised to some degree without detracting from their character. Out of the range, the XK140 is the best all-rounder.

BUYING TIPS

With the newest car coming up to 60 years old, the majority will have been restored by now. This is a costly business to do properly so look for budget rebuilds. The chassis is pretty solid (check for repairs around the suspension) but body rust is everywhere. The XK engine can easily see

200,000 miles if properly maintained, but otherwise it's prone to overheating. Blue smoke and low oil pressure (there should be at least 40psi at 3,000rpm) point to a worn unit, and even the best can leak oil at the crank rear oil seal. There's inherently more slop in the XK120's steering but this can be reduced by XK experts, unlike wheel wobble on this model.

PRICES

Projects start around the £25–30,000 mark but there are few money-making opportunities with one. Roadsters and dropheads are generally worth 80–100 per cent more than fixed-heads and 120s (apart from the rare early aluminium cars) are worth the least. You have to pay at least £75,000 for a good, sound car, although rare aluminium-bodied models are worth £200,000 minimum, with LHD versions lagging not too far behind.

VERDICT

XKs are one of the most desirable 1950s classics around, but you need to try a few to see which model suits you best. There are a number of XK specialists around that will help and it's certainly the safest way to secure a good car at a realistic price

JAGUAR SALOONS

(Historics Auctioneers)

The epitome of a classic British 1960s sports saloon, the Jaguar Mk1 and Mk2 rank high on the wish lists of many enthusiasts, but don't limit yourself with the obvious choices if you want top value.

DATES TO REMEMBER

1955   First Jaguar launched with monocoque construction. XK120 3.4-litre engine downsized to 2,483cc.

1957   3.4 added to range with full-fat 210bhp 3.4-litre engine and all-round disc brakes.

1959   Mk2 launched. For all intents and purposes it's a heavily modified Mk1. A mighty 3.8 flagship followed soon after.

1962   Daimler 2.5 V8 joins range with the SP250 V8 engine, MkX-like interior and automatic transmission only.

1963   S-Type is a Mk2 hull with MkX-style front and rear treatment, plus E-Type independent rear suspension (IRS).

1966   Mk2 (but not Daimler) range downrated with less equipment and cheaper interior. New '420' (also badged as Daimler Sovereign) has MkX-style front, later 4.2-litre engine and better front suspension, steering and brakes.

1967   Mk2 replaced by 240/340 and V8 250; essentially same car identified by slimmer S-type bumpers. 240 gains much more power care of E-Type cylinder head and carbs.

DRIVING

Of the triad, the Mk2 ranks the highest, none more so than the 3.8 with overdrive, yet, with its E-Type rear suspension, the S-type (and 420) is by far the more secure handler – especially compared to the tail happy Mk1. The 220bhp 3.8 still possess GTi-like zeal, but the 210bhp 3.4 is no slouch either, nor is the underrated 240. The Daimler has a disposition of its own that you might like, as do Mk1s which have an entirely different personality to the rest. The unsung hero is the 4.2-litre Jaguar 420 and its Daimler Sovereign equivalent, which sport a torquier engine and a far superior chassis.

BUYING TIPS

Take your time to choose the best one for you – there are many around that are not as good as they look. Check everywhere underneath, especially at the front where the 'crow's feet' structure resides. To restore a Mk1 costs as much as the more popular XK sportsters, and a 2.4 costs exactly the same as a 3.4 to restore without the residual value benefits. The IRS fitted on the S-type/420 has a myriad of bushes which deteriorate and cost around £1,000 to overhaul. Interiors can cost as much as the bodywork to restore and there's even more wood to preserve in a Mk1.

PRICES

Mk2 prices have been stagnating for a number of years and Mk1 values can now match or outstrip them: expect to pay £50,000+ for the cats with the cream, although good 2.4s start from around £20,000, some £10,000 down on a 3.4. The bargain Mk2s are the 240/340, which carry a price similar to the S-type, but nothing beats the 420/Sovereign for getting the most metal for your money, with tidy ones at just £15,000 or less.

VERDICT

There's a classic Jaguar saloon for every taste and budget and the least obvious choice might suit you the best. Take your time and try out as many as you can before finally deciding.

JAGUAR XJ SALOONS

(Author)

Another landmark from William Lyons, the legendary XJ6 is in another league compared to the Mk2 that it replaced, and prices remain considerably cheaper.

DATES TO REMEMBER

1968 Launched to replace existing saloon ranges. The 4.2-litre XK was joined by a new down-sized 2.8. Power-assisted rack-and-pinion steering was standard on all bar the base 2.8.

1969 Daimler Sovereign range duly joins the ranks.

1972 Long-awaited arrival of the 5.3-litre V12, an auto-only saloon, also available in optional long-wheelbase form. A Rolls-rivalling Vanden Plas Double Six becomes the flagship.

1973 Series II introduced with XJC coupé.

1975 Fuel injection for V12 models. XJC hits the showrooms with 4.2- or 5.3-litre engines.

1979 Due to the troubled development of the XJ40 replacement, a stopgap SIII is hurried. Fuel injection for 4.2 and five-speed boxes for 3.4/4.2, along with assorted suspension and running gear upgrades.

1981 XJ12 gained higher efficiency (HE) 'Fireball' cylinder heads for better economy.

1987–92 Last XJ6 made ('87). V12 is converted for lead-free fuel ('89), anti-lock brakes for 1990.

DRIVING

The XJ6 raised the bar so high that even now its driving and refinement levels still greatly impress, as do the ride and handling. The only blot is the traditional over-light power steering that Jaguar insisted upon. The V12 remains a magnificent mile eater, but the base 3.4 is fine for quiet cruising. That said, the much brisker 4.2 is the best overall XJ. Of the strain, the SII is by far the better developed compared to the SI, with the last-of-the-line SIII best of all.

BUYING TIPS

The chief problem with XJs is that their inherently low values have never encouraged expensive care and restorations. There are too many mangy cats on sale as a result, especially the case for SIIs. XJs rust everywhere – terminally underneath. The SIII used a 'long stud' XK engine which was problematic and led to broken studs, failing head gaskets and block-liner trouble. The V12 can last forever, if cared for well. The rear subframe is full of rubber bushes to give that wonderful refinement, but expect them to be worn out. Interiors don't wear well, headlinings are known to sag or collapse and, on XJCs, expect irksome wind noise due to door drop.

PRICES

Prices vary wildly, from under £2,000 for a ropey restoration project and up to £50,000 for a concours SI. Expect slightly less for a V12 saloon. The cheapest of the XJ family is the SII, a result of its reputation for unreliability and poor build – a shame, as a good one is better than any SI. The SII-based XJC used to be unloved and unwanted but now values are the highest of them all.

VERDICT

Perhaps it's the Arthur Daley image but the XJ saloon struggled for a long while to reach deserved classic status, ultimately resulting in their neglect. But a top cat is better to drive and ride in than a rival Rolls-Royce. Yes, really!

JAGUAR E-TYPE

(Author)

Still slinky, sexy and scorching, at 60 years old the E-Type is still the favourite all-time classic car. What more needs to be decided other than which classic 'Coventry Cat' is best for you?

DATES TO REMEMBER

1961 Launched. 3.8 XK150S powered in roadster and coupé styles with the now legendary independent rear suspension (IRS) in all-new monocoque bodyshell.

1964 4.2 replacement comes with larger engine, added torque, new Jaguar gearbox, improved seats and a host of other changes.

1966 2+2 derivative joins range with stretched platform for rear seats and a wider transmission tunnel to also facilitate an automatic option.

1967 Unofficially labelled the Series 1/1/2, it's a unique interim model. The headlamp cowls are deleted but the headlamps remain in the same position.

1968 The proper Series 2 has welcome improvements such as better brakes and seats, while the 2+2 gains a more streamlined look.

1971 S3 has new 276bhp, 5.3-litre V12 sitting on a 10in wheelbase stretch. Improved chassis boasts anti-dive suspension.

1974 Final cars were built; fifty known as Commemorative Editions.

DRIVING

Split temperament best describes the XK/V12 E-Types, but all are wonderfully satisfying in their own way. The former have a more 'vintage' feel, which some enthusiasts want, but for all its bloated appearance, the S3 has better performance, brakes, handling, ride and a much lighter, if feel-less, (powered) steering. It's also the most relaxing, but as a consequence it's more of a GT than the sports car the E-Type started out to be. Purists like the racer 3.8 engine the best, but the 4.2 is more flexible, and it enjoys a slicker gearbox. Unless you carry out a back-to-back test, you'll be hard pressed to tell the difference.

BUYING TIPS

Although sorely tempting, don't buy the first E-Type you come across. Instead, drive a few to get a feel for the car, as they differ due to their age, condition and so on. The vast majority have been restored by now and while some DIY rebuilds are spot on, most aren't. The biggest rust traps are around the tub, chassis sections and particularly the rear-suspension radius-arm mounts. Rear suspension wear means a rebuild will cost in excess of £1,000.

PRICES

Prices are high but have levelled out. Cheapest are the V12 S3s and US repats where you may find a fair example that you can bring back into line for under £30,000. Most average E-Types will hover round the £50,000 mark. American 2+2 autos look tempting as US cars can be valued two-thirds the price of a regular RHD version. The very best matching number RHD cars sell for six figures, with soft tops usually double over what a fixed-head achieves. The S3 V12 is starting to close the gap on the XK versions. Budget as much as £200,000 for an original flat-floor S1 roadster.

VERDICT

The dream classic for so many car lovers, although prices are fast becoming out of reach unless you choose one of the less popular models, like a US import. But at least you'll own an E-Type – which is all that matters, surely?

JAGUAR XK8

With classic curves to spare, the XK8 is much more than a replacement for the stately but elderly XJ-S; it was the embodiment of the E-Type for the new millennium.

DATES TO REMEMBER

1996   XK8 coupé replaces XJ-S. It is still based on the same platform but with E-Type style looks and a new quad-cam, 4-litre V8 coupled to standard automatic transmission. CATS computer-aided suspension is optional, standard on the convertible.

1998   Supercharged XKR introduced: 370bhp, allied to Mercedes auto transmission and standard CATS chassis.

2000   Silverstone special edition (coupé or an XKR convertible). Only 100 are made.

2001   Special launched (another 100 run) squatting on nine-spoke BBS alloy wheels bolted to Brembo brakes.

2002   Larger 4.2-litre engine sees 300bhp for standard XK8 and 400bhp for XKR.

DRIVING

Unlike the XJ-S, the XK8 does go as good as it looks and that V8 really churns out the power, with 290bhp at least. The XKR is simply thrilling and can show its kissing cousin, the Aston DB7, the way home, plus it sports a far superior automatic transmission, with an ingenious J-gate selector design that works almost like a manual. On the other hand, if you don't want outright performance, a standard model, particularly the later 4.2-litre, is quite fast enough and is cheaper to own and maintain. Unlike the XJ-S, there is only a trace of scuttle shake on rough roads with the dropheads.

BUYING TIPS

Like the XJ-S, condition varies enormously and is usually related to price. A service history is important as there were a handful of recalls that should have been attended to. Rust isn't XJ-S terminal but serious enough for you to check underneath: floor, suspension points, bulkheads and sills. Inspect behind the bumpers where electrolytic corrosion can set in between the alloy mounts and steel bolts. The V8 was initially troublesome, suffering from premature bore wear. This was eradicated by 2000, but quad-cam timing gear problems still remain and can cost up to £2,000 to put right. Running-gear wear is confined to front wishbones, wheel bearings (accelerated by wider, grippier tyres), dampers and springs and the E-Type-derived IRS bushes. Try a few XK8s as even a worn one may feel good when it isn't. XK8 specialists advise looking at a 4.2 model as the majority of early cars are not worth bothering with anymore.

PRICES
XK8s can be extremely cheap from £3,000, but you get what you pay for and sorting one out can prove expensive. It is best to budget a minimum of £6,000 for a pampered 'Coventry Cat' with the best (especially XKRs) busting £15,000, and expect the two special editions to become gold-plated classics in the near future. In general, mainstream models are worth less than the equivalent XKR by as much as 50 per cent and cabrios will always fetch more than coupés.

VERDICT
With those E-Type-like looks and performance aplenty, a good XK8 is a superb modern classic that's every bit as good as the not dissimilar but much pricier Aston Martin DB7. One is worth buying with a view to hang on to it.

JAGUAR F-TYPE

(Author)

The long-awaited successor to the legendary E-Type is not only a top cat but, thanks to hefty depreciation, also incredible value for money. It is a good time to use the F-word!

DATES TO REMEMBER
2013   Launched, based upon a shorter, modified XK platform. The roadster came first, employing a supercharged Jaguar 3-litre V6 in 340bhp or the more potent 370bhp V6 S tune, the latter also featuring adaptive suspension and a better interior. Flagship 5-litre V8 requires a special electronic rather than mechanical limited-slip differential to manage the 481bhp deployed. Initially, all F-Types were fitted with an eight-speed automatic transmission.

2014   Coupé (with optional panoramic roof) joins the line-up and the sportier S was rebranded as the R.

2015   Six-speed manual option, while all-wheel drive filtered down to this model at the same time for the V6 S.

2017 Mild facelift and special editions, plus the addition of entry-level 2-litre, four-cylinder turbocharged engine as found in the XE saloons; 296bhp but an automatic only.

DRIVING

On the whole, the F-Type lives up to all the hype. A near-ideal 50/50 weight distribution aided by adaptive damping on the V6 S and V8 R, the F-Type possesses a thoroughbred sports-car poise and agility while four-wheel drive adds astonishing grip and security into the mix. All engines – including the 'four' – make for scalded cats, so much so that it's becoming generally accepted that the V6 S is the best all-rounder.

BUYING TIPS

When new, special service packages were popular options. Are any still active? Similarly, the standard three-year warranty could be extended for up to five years – another welcome bonus. There's no traditional service history book, all the info is contained on dealer databases. Early cars suffered a number of major recalls. Worn bearings and cranks and oil-pump failures on the V6 are not unknown, although this engine is regarded as more trustworthy than the V8. The Jaguar F-Type Owners' Club and F-Type forums are invaluable places to join to check what owners are experiencing.

PRICES

Being modern, hefty depreciation ensures spectacular value for money, with the bottom line being £25,000, particularly if it's a basic V6, although the general start price can be upwards of £30,000. Specs, optional extras, whether it's AWD and colours (whites are becoming unfashionable, unlike grey, red and black) have a significant impact on prices. There are a lot more V6 models on the market and the general standard of cars is pretty good. Jaguar's 'Approved Used' programme is regarded as one of the best around with a no-claims limit and an unlimited-mileage, two-year warranty. Two-year breakdown assistance is also thrown in.

VERDICT

Costing £60,000 when new, you now buy one easily for less than half the original showroom price. However, there are enough running faults to advise anyone wanting an F-Type to exercise considerable caution when buying one.

JAGUAR XJ-S

(Author)

A GT as opposed to a sports car, this misunderstood E-Type replacement has at last gained deserved classic status and remains remarkable value for money.

DATES TO REMEMBER

1975   Launched based on a shortened XJ6 platform, and powered by the now familiar 5.3 V12.

1981   At the behest of owners' clubs, a greatly revised XJ-S, gaining traditional wood and leather interior and chrome bumpers, is launched, equipped with a modified, fuel-injected V12 engine called HE (High Efficiency) to improve economy.

1983   Long-awaited all-new Jaguar engine is a straight-six 3.6-litre with either a Getrag five-speed manual or ZF four-speed automatic.

1984   Quirkily styled two-seat cabriolet (XJ-SC) with a novel rear folding hood section, designed by Tickford, is launched.

1988   Strange-looking SC is dropped in favour of a proper convertible. Anti-lock brakes are added to the package.

1991   Facelift includes tidier styling and revised interior. AJ6 engine grows to 4.0 litres with 233bhp. XJ-S nomenclature changed to a simpler XJS badge.

1993   V12 grows to 6.0 litres. Unliked inboard rear disc brakes are moved outboard. Also 2+2 seating is squeezed into the convertible.

1996   Final Commemorative and Celebration run-out models made.

DRIVING

It's not an E-Type. But once you accept this you'll find the XJ-S an exceptional GT that performs better than it looks, in no small part due to the excellence of the XJ6 platform, save from the traditional Jag failing of an over-light power steering. Performance isn't an issue, with the six-cylinder models performing as well as the V12 (4-litre especially), yet are a lot more economical. The XJ-S is none too roomy but no worse than its main rivals, and you can't knock the Jaguar for its comfort or refinement.

BUYING TIPS

Because the XJ-S was never regarded as a classic, neglect and skipped servicing has always plagued the car, and you must be ultra-careful when buying as many aren't as good as they look.

Rust runs riot over the entire body, and pre-1982 cars will be rotten as the build quality was poor. Facelifted cars of the 1990s are the best bets for a variety of reasons, although some experts claim that 1991–93 were the worst years due to cheaper steel being used. Leaky rear axles commonly spew lube over the brakes, while the interior can easily look tatty with tired trim and drooping headlinings common.

PRICES

Prices vary wildly and you get what you pay for, but the good news is that XJ-S standards are rising. Budget no less than £5,000 for something worth owning, but even then it will require work such as an IRS overhaul, air-conditioning rectification, replacement headlining and a new radiator. At the top end, the last-of-the-line Celebration convertibles can hit £40,000; coupés are typically around 30–40 per cent cheaper. You need around £10,000 to own something remotely worth having. SCs come in and out of favour.

VERDICT

With standards and prices on the up, the XJ-S is now as accepted as a true Browns Lane classic and the time to buy is now. It doesn't have the character of an E-Type, but this doesn't make the XJ-S a lesser car by a long chalk.

JAGUAR XK

Sandwiched between the capable XK8 and the exciting new F-Type, the XK is arguably the best of the three, providing tremendous driver appeal and spectacular value for money.

DATES TO REMEMBER

2006   New aluminium-constructed XK range succeeds XK8 with new chassis and an up-gunned V8 engine, initially as a 4.2, with the more potent XKR also available.

2008   XK60 special edition celebrates 60 years of the famous XK name.

2009   Facelifted XK boasts sharper looks and packs an all-new 5-litre V8; 380bhp nominally and more than 500bhp in XKR tune.

DRIVING

Compared to the XJS-derived XK8, the XK is a whole new ball game. If the XK8 was seen as an Aston Martin DB7 alternative then the XK is a viable DB9 substitute, boasting an equally impressive ride/handling balance, with Jaguar's excellent CATS adaptive suspension, fitted to the majority, assisting here. Unless you're a speed freak or want to partake in track days, the higher-tune XKR seems a bit pointless on our roads, although the scintillating XKR-S will become a sure-fire classic. Where the XK stands head and shoulders above the long awaited F-Type is in its far more accommodating, comfy cockpit that offers some semblance of practicality, with the coupé rekindling fond memories of the E-Type thanks to its side-opening rear hatch door.

BUYING TIPS

Aluminium build, so rust isn't an issue as such. However, alloy panels corrode readily once the paint is scratched, and check the wheel arches for bubbling. Footwells can fill with water if the air-con drain tube is blocked. So long as the CATS adaptive suspension is working, there's little to fret over. Damaged alloys are not the small matter you may envisage if they can't be refurbished. The now well-proven V8 engine should be okay, and as timing gear is chain driven, few problems are now experienced but check anyway. There were a few dealer recalls so check with the service history, and be aware of a variety of electrical issues, one involving the 'smart' ignition key.

PRICES

XKs are still depreciating although levelling out – so the newer the car, the more it's going to shed value. An early high-mileage though sound XK can be yours for under £10,000. This is unbelievable value even if you add some £2,500 more for a convertible, which is roughly what a well-used XKR coupé retails for. The last 2016 cars sell for well under £35,000 and these values will fall pretty dramatically. A Portfolio edition, which also came out in May 2006 with every creature comfort you could possibly want, may be worth a bit extra, though.

VERDICT

The XK is Jaguar's 'DB9' and in many respects it's the far better car, as well as being considerably more affordable. Not only that, the Jag is a far more accommodating tourer than its F-Type replacement. A modern classic for sure.

JENSEN 541 AND C-V8

(Historics Auctioneers)

This Jensen grand tourer can be regarded as an Austin-Healey but for all the family to enjoy in comfort, and is as easy to own and run. The C-V8 is a cut-price Aston eater.

DATES TO REMEMBER

1953   Initial designs announced, a highbrow fibreglass-bodied GT using the big 4-litre Austin Princess engine.

1955   Cars now reach customers with a tuned 117bhp engine.

1956   541 DeLuxe debuts at the London Motor Show, now with all-round disc brakes.

1957   541R is more performance orientated, relying on the Princess (DS7) limousine's six-cylinder, twin-carb engine for 140bhp.

1960   541S is the first facelifted model, sprouting more length and width for added interior space and comfort.

1962   Aggressive looking C-V8 replacement is 541 based but now powered by a Chrysler Golden Commando 5.9-litre, 305bhp Chrysler V8 engine.

1963   Mk2 facelift includes a 6.3-litre V8 packing 330bhp. Armstrong Selectaride dampers are also standard.

DRIVING

If you want something fast, fleet, luxurious and comfortable that is decidedly distinctive, these Jensens could be just the ticket. The 541 is quite Healey-like to drive, although the Jensen is far more comfortable and quieter with surprising fuel economy. The C-V8 takes an entirely different persona and can match any Aston Martin in the performance stakes, with a fabulous American V8 growl into the bargain. Handling on all cars is good for their era, although the all-disc-braked models are notably superior if you drive hard.

BUYING TIPS

Thanks to specialists like Martin Robey, the spares situation is surprisingly good. The fibreglass is of good quality; it's the chassis that sends many Jensens to the scrapheap. Sill condition is critical. Mechanically, it's Big Healey tough and the American V8s can rack up massive mileages, plus spare parts for the Chrysler units are freely available, especially in the US. Transmissions and running gear (some of it shared by the Healey) pose few problems, although it's unlikely that the Armstrong adjustable damping system (altered from inside the car) is still operative. The rack-and-pinion steering on the S has a bespoke rack that's impossible to replace so it can only be overhauled if worn out.

PRICES

In line with later Interceptors, values have soared over the past couple of years and the best cars can achieve well over £60,000, with the C-V8 generally worth an extra £10–15,000. Good-to-tidy examples are valued at £50,000 (all models) with projects worth around £20,000, although restoration costs are extremely high, especially if the GRP body requires extensive fettling.

VERDICT

While all eyes are now on Interceptors, these earlier Jensens are worth considering for the same money, enjoying more exclusivity as well as a Healey-like character. The 541R is the 541 to go for, but any C-V8 is worth owning.

JENSEN INTERCEPTOR

(Historics Auctioneers)

Known as the Birmingham Ferrari, care of its Aston-like pace and personality plus prestige that would do a Bentley proud, the suave Interceptor was the choice of numerous celebrities.

DATES TO REMEMBER

1966/7   Interceptor/4x4 FF replaces CV-8 using its running gear but clothed with a stylish new sports hatch body from Touring of Italy.

1969   SII integrates with many refinements including standard power steering and better ventilation. Director is a special spin off with a built in typewriter sited in the glovebox.

1971   Four-wheel-drive FF is dropped.

1972   SIII adopts Chrysler's meaty 7.2-litre V8 and known as the SP (six pack, thanks to the number of carbs fitted) pumping out 385bhp.

1974   Engine slightly detuned and a suave drophead introduced, as well as an odd-looking booted version. Jensen ceased producing cars in 1976, although production briefly restarted in 1982.

DRIVING

The Interceptor is a stylish, speedy supercar yet with a practical slant thanks to its glass hatch and roomy cabin. With a nominal 325bhp and 425lb ft of torque, the Jensen is still a very quick car indeed. The 7.2 V8 isn't really any faster and some serial owners actively prefer the more agile nature of the 6.3. The 385bhp SP may be the most muscular, but its odd vacuum throttle characteristics are disliked by many. Handling is generally good and while the FF is no Audi Quattro, there are few modern classics that have the Jensen's security, although all Interceptors are better suited to long-distance high-speed touring. There aren't many Interceptors that are still standard spec, but that's no bad thing because they weren't that well further developed over their production run.

BUYING TIPS

The perennial problem with these Jensens stems from their historically low values and Aston-priced restoration costs, which led to many seriously neglected 'superbangers', although this is fast changing. Ruinous rust is the main worry plus chassis-tube rot on the FF is serious as the tubes also act as vacuum chambers for the brakes ... Mechanically, the car is utterly conventional and tough although expect sloppy suspensions.

PRICES

Not that long ago a Jensen could be yours for not much over £10,000. Now, they regularly sell for over ten times this, and in the case of the FFs, over £200,000. Beware of anything advertised under £35,000 as it will require a lot of expensive work. Convertibles command at least £15,000 above a normal coupé. If you are paying top-dollar prices, you may want to look at the re-engineered, reborn alternatives such as the Interceptor R from Jensen International Automotive, which rely on modern running gear and brawny Chevrolet engines plus modern 4x4 systems if desired.

VERDICT

Interceptors took a long time to achieve their justly deserved classic status, yet even at their escalated prices, a good one is still a bit of a bargain when compared to an equivalent Aston or Jaguar – and is as good to own.

JENSEN-HEALEY

(Historics Auctioneers)

With famous names such as Lotus, Sunbeam and Jensen all involved in making an all-new Healey for the 1970s, this sports car has all the right ingredients to become a legend.

DATES TO REMEMBER

1972   All-new Healey for the 1970s relies on Lotus power, Sunbeam transmission and Vauxhall running gear. It was styled by Aston Martin stylist William Towns, with Jensen putting it all together.

1973   A heavily revised Mk2 for 1974 is identified by a side styling strip and new wheels, plus the interior is made plusher with more soundproofing. Mechanically, the changes centred around a better sorted Lotus engine and a Getrag five-speed 'box.

1975   Jensen GT is the result of Healey leaving the project and the roadster evolving into a luxurious sports hatch to rival the Reliant Scimitar GTE. Fewer than 500 are made.

DRIVING

Build and reliability issues aside, the Jensen-Healey was the best British sports car of the 1970s, possessing fine driving manners and one of the most accommodating and ergonomic sports-car cockpits around. Although a trifle soft-riding to appease the US market, handling is still very good and the J-H feels far more modern than any MGB or TR, even if stiffer dampers are now advised. The Jensen-Healey was the logical development of those much-loved British classics but is better suited to today's roads, possessing better crash protection. While a bit rough and ready, the Lotus 16-valve engine, designed for the Esprit, is no mean performer and its 140bhp will blow any TR6 away, and later models came with five-speed transmissions.

BUYING TIPS

Chassis-leg rust is not only an MOT failure but also an involved repair, as a full front-end strip – engine, gearbox, front suspension – is required if it is to be done right. Serious corrosion can spread to the floors, requiring a major rebuild. The Chrysler Rapier gearbox is weak and parts aren't exactly plentiful. The running gear is Vauxhall Viva-derived and reliable, but the Lotus engine is a bugbear. Original units were notoriously fragile and prone to leaks but thankfully were much improved for the Mk2. The Jensen-Healey Preservation Society is a good website to visit. As most went to the States, you can not only pick up rot-free models more easily but Jensen-Healey Parts & Spares of America offers a strong parts and tuning gear supply.

PRICES

Lack of interest due to a poor reputation contrived to keep prices at rock bottom for years and it's only fairly recently that values have risen. Nevertheless, even the best Jensen-Healey, which has to be the Mk2, will rarely break the £15,000 barrier and most sell at between £6,000 and £9,000. Condition counts more than whether it's a MkI or MkII, although the GT's rarity (fewer than 500 made) increases their stock by around £1,000–£2,000.

VERDICT

The Jensen-Healey is certainly on the cusp of becoming a cult classic. If you want one at a bargain price, buy one before the market wakes up to what this fine pedigree-packed sports car has to offer.

LAMBORGHINI GALLARDO

The Lamborghini Gallardo is one of the most accessible, usable and surprisingly affordable Italian supercars around. It also has one of the most evocative names in the business.

DATES TO REMEMBER

2003   Launched to become the most popular Lamborghinis ever made by a long stretch. Relies on German Audi (R8) hardware including its 500bhp V10 engine harnessed by Quattro all-wheel drive with a manual or semi-automatic option, all wrapped in stunning sharp-suited styling.

2006   Revisions majoring on increased performance with an extra 20bhp, slightly lower gearing and sportier sounding exhaust, complimented by a tweaked suspension incorporating a new steering rack. Drophead Gallardo Spyder is also introduced along with special-edition Gallardo SE, of which only 250 were made.

2008   L560-4 is evolution model with 5.2-litre 552bhp engine.

DRIVING

For a fully fledged Italian supercar, the Gallardo is amazingly user-friendly, due in no small part to the fitment of Audi's Quattro four-wheel-drive system to control the Audi R8 engine that kicks out a nominal 500bhp for shattering, Porsche 911 Turbo-beating performance. Compared to the R8, the Lamborghini is on another performance level, yet when you are in a more relaxed mood, it easily doubles up as a civilised tourer. The automated manual gearbox option (e-gear) does need some familiarising to get the best out of it.

BUYING TIPS

The car's honesty is paramount so verify with an HPI check to see whether it has been crash repaired – important as they are popular for track days. By the same token, a valid Lamborghini service history is crucial. Trusted independents are fine, however, and can keep service prices down to a highly reasonable £550. Suspensions suffer from hard driving and track days, especially the bushes and ball joints, with the brakes suffering similarly. The sign of a good, well-cared-for car is if correct type replacements are fitted as well as the right tyres; speak to a Lamborghini expert or lamborghiniownersclub.co.uk about this. Apart from failed ignition coil packs, the Audi engine is inherently strong and long-lasting but less so the gearboxes. Clutches wilt under hard use and cost around £2,500 to fix plus the quirky e-gear system has troubles of its own, such as poor gear-changes and failing actuators.

PRICES

Costing £160,000 at launch, a fair number of the 15,000 made reside in the UK, with prices now starting around £60,000 for a high-mileage early model or, more likely, around £75,000 for the better-looked-after cars coming from a specialist or main dealer and backed by a worthy warranty. Six-figure price tags are not uncommon for the limited and special editions as well as the Spyder dropheads. There's no shortage of Gallardos on the market so shop around and if possible drive a few to ascertain a reliable benchmark, as their conditions vary and even hard-driven high milers will feel out of this world to the Gallardo novice.

VERDICT

One of the best modern supercars due to its practical, usable nature, but for peace of mind purchase from a good specialist. And use it regularly as long periods of inactivity will do it (and you!) more harm than good.

LANCIA MONTECARLO

(Historics Auctioneers)

Montecarlo is a Lancia which can pass off as a Ferrari thanks to its pretty Pininfarina shape, exquisite mid-engine handling, adequate performance and typical Italian flair.

DATES TO REMEMBER

1975   Launched at the Geneva Motor Show, originally as Fiat design X/20 to complement the similar-in-concept X/19, before being farmed out to Lancia, sharing the Beta 2-litre saloon's engine, transmission and all-round MacPherson strut suspension.

1977   Badged Montecarlo for the UK with choice of fixed roof or (a no cost option) foldback Spider alternative. Rear buttress look is changed.

1978   Production suspended to sort out the seriously over-sensitive lock-prone brakes which blighted the design.

1980   Series 2 relaunch comes with better brakes, better chassis and 14in wheels while the engine gains a Magneti Marelli electronic ignition system. Discontinued in 1984.

DRIVING

The Montecarlo is really big brother to the sweet little Fiat X1/9, enjoying more performance and cockpit space twinned with the look of a Ferrari about it. In fact, the Lancia, like the X1/9, can be likened to a baby Ferrari and is certainly a rarer sight on the road. With sublime handling, the Montecarlo has it all – apart from decent brakes, which is why it was dropped while Lancia sorted the trouble out. This culminated in revisions to the front discs and servo arrangement, making the S2 far safer to drive in the wet, although many SIs have been adapted by now. As a tourer the Lancia is nicely accommodating and better than the X1/9 or a Lotus Europa, although it is still a rather noisy GT.

BUYING TIPS

There are not many left in the UK, but you still need to be picky as condition differs greatly. Rot, as with all Betas, is terminal, but post-1981 cars are better rustproofed, it's said, although check for cracking subframes as well. The engine, if the timing belts and tensioner are renewed periodically, is fairly bullet proof, and the rest of the car holds no horrendous vices apart from the rear hubs, which are Fiat X1/9 items and are hard to obtain. The Monte Hospital (www. montehospital. co.uk) is the place to go for spares and advice.

PRICES

A cut-price Ferrari 308? Montecarlo values are on the up, but still the very best are unlikely to break £20,000 with good honest alternatives, albeit needing TLC, for half this. Of the 7,500 made up to 1984, around 1,000 were destined for our shores and perhaps only 200 remain, in various states of despair, but LHD examples remain fairly plentiful. However, steer clear of US cars as they use tepid 1.8 power and are not as nice to drive by half.

VERDICT

Vastly underrated for too long, Montecarlos are great cut-price pseudo supercars, and don't forget the Beta Spider, which is a 2+2 based on the coupé with a targa roof and folding rear section, and even cheaper, from around £6,000.

LANCIA INTEGRALE

With its unique blend of supercar performance and tenacious 4x4 grip that beats even an Audi Quattro, the Integrale is an equally legendary rally car but with hatchback practicality.

DATES TO REMEMBER

1984   The Integrale story starts with the Delta HF, fitted with a 1.6 140bhp engine and front-wheel drive only.

1985   New 2-litre twin-cam 'four' for 185bhp is forerunner to the Integrale, called the Delta HF Turbo, with all-wheel drive following a year later.

1988   'Real' Delta Integrale arrives, with its aggressive boxy wheel arches. A bigger turbocharger and intercooler sorts the power out.

1989   New 16-valve engine raises power to 200bhp and the fixed torque split is now 47:53 front to rear. A new lowered suspension also features.

1991   Evoluzione (aka Evo 1) appears with an even more aggressive look and 210bhp, and the car's rear wing is adjustable.

1992   A year for special editions. A series of 400 Integrales are made featuring Martini Racing colours, with a run of 310 special editions featuring white paintwork with a Martini Racing stripe along the flanks.

1993   Evoluzione 2 launched. Last of the range is marked with a number of Special Edition cars to celebrate: Giallo, BlueLagos, Pearl White, Dealer Edition and Final Edition.

DRIVING

Fantastic is the only way to describe how a good Integrale drives because, unless you're used to driving supercars, you'll be blown away by the car's dynamic abilities some thirty-five years on. It's not so much the usable performance that impresses but the way it puts the power down, posting phenomenal cross-country speeds in safety thanks to a wonderful chassis. What's more, all this supercar ability doesn't come at the expense of practicality as there's room for five with their luggage, although being LHD will be a hindrance for some. Don't overlook the plainer, milder Delta HF and GT ranges. Yes, they are slower and some are front-drive only, but in their day they were thrilling drives.

BUYING TIPS

Integrity and provenance are the watchwords. Crashed and thrashed Integrales are rife. Check the V5c for the number of past owners for starters. Is the car original? Rust can be an issue so check sills and inner rear wings, rear crossmember and rear suspension turrets. Being a rally winner, the Integrale is tough, but if cornered hard with low oil in the sump, the big-end bearings will be starved of lube.

PRICES

Like the rival RS Escort Cosworth, prices have gone through the roof, and if you want the best then expect to pay £50,000 for an Evo2 and more for a special edition model. Good, sound, honest if hardly concours Evos cost around £35,000, but older Delta HF Turbos can be had for around £20,000 or less, with Delta HFs and 1600GTs perhaps a quarter of this.

VERDICT

With Ferrari-like performance, the cornering ability and grip of a Group B rally car yet room for all the family and their luggage, the Lancia Integrale is quite unique. But don't ignore the lesser Lancias which are considerably cheaper.

LAND ROVER

(Author)

Still the definitive off-roader for many, the legendary Land Rover is more a way of life for some enthusiasts who wouldn't be without theirs.

DATES TO REMEMBER

1948   First pre-production cars made.

1951   The 1,600cc engine is replaced with a brawnier 2-litre unit.

1953   Standard wheelbase is upped to 86 inches and a long-wheelbase (107in) edition is also introduced for those needing more space.

1957   A 2-litre diesel is offered.

1958   Series II introduced.

1961   Series IIA has an upgraded 2.2-litre diesel engine.

1971   Series III boasts much improved interior, and an all-synchromesh gearbox is now fitted.

1979   Range Rover 3.5-litre petrol V8 supersedes old six-cylinder 2.6-litre option.

1983   Series III is replaced by the 110 (and from '84 also the 90), with a five-speed gearbox, servo-assisted front disc brakes and coil-spring suspension.

1990   Defender is a new name although vehicle is little different from the outgoing 90 and 110, but power steering is now standard, plus the diesel becomes the 200 TDI 2.5-litre unit.

1993   300 TDI 2.5-litre five-cylinder engine is now used, mated to a better five-speed gearbox.

1998   Discovery TD5 engine replaces old 300 TDI unit. Electronic traction control plus anti-lock brakes now figure.

2006   All change with a Ford-derived 2.4 TDCi engine together with six-speed gearbox and a revised interior.

DRIVING

There's nothing like a Land Rover to drive, but will you like one? They are essentially heavy-duty, industrial, all-weather off roaders that pander little to refinement. Early ones (Series I/II) are for the diehard collectors only as they are such hard work to drive over long distances. The Series III of the 1970s is far more usable but still not exactly civilised, so if you want to use one regularly, consider a 90/110 or perhaps a Defender with their coil-spring suspension. The later the car the more usable it is, particularly the diesels, and the TD5, taken from the Discovery, is ideal.

BUYING TIPS

Owner support is superb either from the factory or independent specialists and owners' clubs, the latter also offering a brilliant social scene. Landies are naturally used hard, but check chassis for arduous off-road use and major rust. The later TDIs can be problematic, blowing head gaskets and holing pistons, and many may have a later Discovery unit installed instead. The old Rover petrol units are fine and spares aren't a major problem; V8s are great if thirsty and dislike infrequent oil changes.

PRICES

There is something for everybody. You can cheerfully pay as much as £40,000 for a mint Series I (but because of their status they can only rise in value), yet a project Series II can still be picked up for just £2,000 or less. The 110 is a logical buy for most folk but are less sought after by hard-core off-roaders. At the other end of the market, you can purchase the last-of-the-line examples for around £35,000.

VERDICT

If you are up to it, a Land Rover makes a fantastic all-weather 24/7 classic that you can put to work as a second runabout. Once you've had one they become part of the family, but do protect yours as Land Rover theft is rife.

RANGE ROVER

The 4x4 that brought off-roaders into the city to evolve into prestige status symbols, Range Rovers are multi-tasking marvels and working classics that can earn their keep.

DATES TO REMEMBER

1970   Launched as an upmarket, three-door shooting brake, V8-powered Land Rover. Skin panels are mostly aluminium, fitted to a steel base, sited on a strong welded box-section ladder chassis.

1973   Revisions see added luxury such as cloth trim and carpeting while power steering, at last, becomes optional.

1982   Chrysler Torqueflite three-speed automatic becomes available.

1983   Rover SD1 five-speed gearbox with a new transfer gearbox plus trim upgrades announced.

1985 Vogue gains Rover SD1 fuel-injected engine while the chassis is uprated.

1986 Italian VM Turbodiesel option. A new Borg Warner chain-drive 4x4 set-up is fitted.

1990 V8 is enlarged to 3.9-litres while the VM diesel is also uprated. ABS is standard on Vogue SE and optional on the rest.

1992 Longer-wheelbase LSE variant introduced. V8 is now 4.2-litres and Italian VM diesel is replaced by a Land Rover design.

1994 Original Range Rover stays on and called the Classic as the all-new high-tech P38 replacement takes over.

2002 Known as L322, the Range Rover ditches a chassis for a unitary body plus new BMW V8s and straight six engines.

DRIVING

There are three generations and all have different attributes. Original Range Rovers are not dissimilar to Land Rovers, albeit with far better handling, more luxury, comfort and refinement (especially air-suspension models) on the road yet still peerless off it. With production running over a quarter of a century, it stands to reason that the later the model, the better and easier it is to drive. The underrated P38 has more room and civility, and the BMW turbodiesels are excellent. The L322 is something else, and thanks to their outstanding handling and ride, quickly became regarded more as an off-road limousine than a working 4x4.

BUYING TIPS

Range Rovers don't wear particularly well and the original models rust badly, especially the chassis frame, so don't be surprised to discover past repairs. The stalwart of a V8 is generally tough and durable with parts both affordable and attainable. VM diesels aren't well liked plus spares supply isn't good. The P38 was dogged by poor build and unreliability, ruining its reputation and residuals. The L322 also needs a serious think as its electronics are dubious at best.

PRICES

The bargains are the P38s, where £5,000 will net you a decent model – you can purchase one for half this but you'd be asking for trouble. Likewise, cheap L322s are huge liabilities and you need to spend as much as you can to avoid big trouble, £10,000 at least. Original Range Rovers vary greatly in price and pristine three-door models can command well in excess of £50,000.

VERDICT

With such a wide choice and price span, there's a Range Rover with your name on it. A good one makes for a marvellous working classic, but you must exercise great care when purchasing to avoid expensive mistakes.

LOTUS ELAN

(Historics Auctioneers)

A landmark in sports-car design, the lovely little Lotus Elan is a driver's delight that performs as well as it looks and, thanks to specialist support, is easier to own than when new.

DATES TO REMEMBER

1962 Launched, powered by a 109bhp Lotus-developed 1,558cc twin-cam engine via a Ford transmission and Triumph Spitfire front suspension and steering.

1964 Series 2 features larger front brake callipers and full-width wooden dashboard.

1965 Series 3 coupé has a closer-ratio gearbox, longer boot lid and a boot-mounted battery.

1966 Optional Special Equipment includes 115bhp engine, an even-closer-ratio gearbox and servo-assisted brakes. S3 convertible introduced with the same spec as the coupé.

1967 Longer, wider four-seater Plus 2 is fixed-head only with 118bhp to restore the performance of this heavier offshoot.

1968 Elan Series 4 has a reported fifty amendments. Plus 2S, boasting an even plusher trim, replaces the Plus 2.

1971 Elan Sprint is ultimate, packing 126bhp from new big-valve engine, stronger transmission and two-tone paint. Similar-engined +2S 130 sports an optional five-speed gearbox.

DRIVING

The Elan proved that sports cars could be driven with fingertip finesse rather than needing to be hauled by the scruff of the neck like traditional roadsters needed to be. A standard setter, yet if anything the wider-track Plus 2 is the better handler, say some Lotus experts. Elan has its faults, mind, such as a flimsy feel, and all are rather frantic at speed so are not the best of cruisers despite a comfortable ride. Also, unless modern driveshafts are now fitted, the original design leads to 'kangarooing' until the right throttle technique is learned.

BUYING TIPS

Rarely do two Elans drive the same, so test as many as you can to set a benchmark. Does the car run straight? Despite their age and simplicity, they can need a specialist to restore correctly. Chassis frailty is well known so look for rust and patch repairs. A new galvanised chassis may be the best solution at around £10,000 fitted. Look for smoke and worn timing chains (is its adjuster screwed right in?). Overheating can be a problem, along with failed water pumps and oil leaks. At the rear, failed driveshafts are common. Five-speed gearboxes used Austin Maxi internals, which are frail and now hard to source for repair parts.

PRICES

While now soaring in value, Plus2s will always be worth less than a normal Elan although, apart from the Sprints, there's comparative price uniformity across the board. Priciest are the early S1/S2 (for historic motorsport reasons) and later Sprints which can carry £50,000+ tickets if nigh on showroom fresh, and the £100,000 Elan isn't far away. Otherwise, good usable models hover around £35,000, with Sprints generally carrying a £5–£10,000 premium and Plus 2s usually trailing by £5,000.

VERDICT

The car which found fame in *The Avengers* still has M-appeal, but it requires frequent attention to keep reliable. Run one like an MGB or MX-5 and the well-worn acronym 'Lots Of Trouble, Usually Serious' may rear its head!

LOTUS ELAN SE

(MagicCarPics)

Unlike the Mazda MX-5 retro clone, when Lotus wanted a new Elan it went completely the other way. It's now one of the most affordable and durable Lotuses ever made.

DATES TO REMEMBER

1989   All-new eagerly awaited Elan (M100) is announced using 1.6-litre Isuzu engine and transmission, an advanced suspension design and front-wheel drive. SE model has turbocharged 165bhp engine. Slow sales and high price tags result in the model being dropped as early as 1992.

1994   Now under the stewardship of Bugatti, the S2 is relaunched with many modifications, which include a modified chassis, larger tyres and a catalysed turbo engine but only 800 S2s are made.

DRIVING

A complete contrast to the original, which was copied heavily by Mazda for its best-selling MX-5, the wedge-shaped Elan SE is the first front-wheel-drive sports car, but not that you'd know it for most of the time. So precise and secure is the car's highly praised handling that thirty years on, it is still regarded as one of the finest-handling front-wheel-drive cars ever – a GTi sports car, in fact. Typically Lotus, the ride is quite exceptional and in terms of usability and civility the M100 is streets ahead of the original classic. The Isuzu engine may lack the pedigree and sporting character of the classic Lotus unit, but it delivers the goods with the SE as quick as the Elan Sprint.

BUYING TIPS

The M100 is probably the most reliable Lotus ever built, which means mechanically you have little to worry about. Pay particular attention to the front and rear suspension arms on early cars because being of steel, they rust accordingly. S2s use galvanised parts which can be fitted. Also check for chassis damage due to incorrect jacking. Replacement chassis parts and frames are available, as are new bodies, at a price. The 'clamshell' bodywork is of good quality and only neglected cars will show it, although red can fade badly to pink, and British Racing Green can highlight panel defects. The interior is not so durable with sagging leather trim, aged door and window seals (which can cost up to £700 to rectify), hood leaks, misted-up instrument binnacles and general wear is common.

PRICES

This Elan ranks as one the most affordable Lotuses around, despite values rising due to the car's increasing fanbase. It's hard to spend more than £15,000 for a super SE and the general guide is between £8–£10,000 with S2s attracting a small price premium. It's hard to value a non-turbo car but by rights it should sell for much less because they aren't as desirable, but, on the other hand, their sheer rarity may well come to the fore in the future.

VERDICT

The M100 has a unique character for a sports car more akin to a GTi convertible, which split opinions. However, there's no argument about the car's shattering point-to-point pace, excellent durability and super value for money.

LOTUS ESPRIT

The sensational mid-engine Esprit sells on looks alone. But it's also a fantastic driver's car. A favourite with James Bond, but take care when diving in at the deep end with this supercar ...

DATES TO REMEMBER

1975   Announced powered by new Lotus 16V 160bhp 1,973cc engine using first-generation Opel Manta front suspension.

1978   S2 has improved interior, Speedline wheels. Commemorating American Mario Andretti becoming F1 World Champion, 147 JPS black and gold special editions are marketed.

1980   Engine upped to 2,174cc. New high-power Esprit Turbo has 210bhp. Opel suspension is replaced by the Triumph system previously used by Lotus.

1981   S3 features the same chassis and suspension as the Turbo version, the latter becoming a production model.

1987   X180 is a clever reskin and a 'pseudo' S4. Renault transaxle replaces old Citroën SM one.

1991   SE gains anti-lock brakes, before 'proper' S4 replacement after a production run of more than 1,500.

1993   Esprit Sport 300 is a 300bhp road racer identified by a special plaque to prove its authenticity.

1996   Basic S4 dropped (622 made). S4S packs 280bhp.

1998   V8-powered Esprit posts 350bhp. SE replaces GT3.

1999   The Sport 350 is little more than a stripped-out V8 and only fifty-four are made.

DRIVING

Thanks to its exalted chassis, few moderns can keep station with a well-maintained, spiritedly driven Esprit, even if their Range Rover-like width means there's precious road room on hand when this Lotus starts to break adhesion. The S1 is a roughneck, but the S2 and especially S3 are far better bets, not least because the 2.2-litre engine's increased torque and improved refinement are worth having. The S4 range is almost a different car to the original, with much higher ambitions (up to 300bhp) and superb driving manners.

BUYING TIPS

There's a whole gamut of Esprits so take time to sift through the ranges to pick the right one. Despite an aged design, Esprits still demand expert care, particularly the rear suspension's geometry; drive a few as standards vary worryingly. The body fibreglass is strong and cracking and crazing rarely occur, but look for accident damage. Properly maintained, the Lotus engine should be long-lasting, unlike the V8, as wonderful as it is.

PRICES

Because of the Bond Esprit making such a splash, S1s command the most dosh – over £70,000 for the best examples, especially if it's an Essex Turbo – despite the S2 and S3 being far better cars at around half the price, say £20,000 for a fair example. Good 'proper' S4s start from under £30,000, and double this for a Sport 300 or the V8, although Sport 350s are gold dust at £50–£60,000+. Bargain Esprits are the halfway-house S4 'X180' and can sell for as little as £11,000.

VERDICT

The first genuine Lotus supercar can be a bargain buy if you choose the right model and buy on condition not price. The S1 has the most classic kudos about it, but the S4 is by far the better-developed Esprit.

LOTUS CORTINA

(Author)

This legendary Cortina was in production when Lotus-Ford ruled the race tracks with legends such as Clark, Hill and Stewart at the helm. It's the most coveted Cortina of all time.

DATES TO REMEMBER

1963   Announced that January but not launched until the summer, Lotus Cortina followed the Cortina 1500GT but was far more advanced thanks to aluminium panels, Elan running gear and a radical coil-spring rear suspension, plus it weighed some 20kg less than the donor 1200 deluxe.

1964   As the Cortina was revised so was the Lotus, here benefiting from smarter frontal and interior. Fewer alloy panels were being used in the car's production and the gearbox ratios were revised.

1965   A special 115bhp Equipment variant was announced, but after too many rear-axle failures, the simpler rear suspension of the GT was substituted.

1967   Following on from the launch of the Mk2 Cortina in late '66, the new Lotus Cortina is announced using the famous Corsair '2000E' gearbox and a 109bhp engine tuned to counter the added weight. By the year's end the iconic Lotus badges were replaced by 'Twin Cam' to align with similar-engined Escort Twin Cam.

DRIVING

Chalk and cheese can describe these two fast Fords. Simply put, the Mk1 enjoys the more sporting, almost road-racer-like character that you expect from a Lotus. The Mk2 feels more like a Cortina, albeit one fitted with a Lotus engine rather than enjoying its own special personality, although it is the most rounded and refined. The first Mk1s with their infamous A-frame coil-spring rear suspension are for the purist as it's generally regarded that the simpler 1965 GT set-up works best, allowing the rear to slide easier.

BUYING TIPS

First of all, is it genuine? Counterfeit Lotus Cortinas were widespread in their day and are still passed off as the real thing. All Mk1s should carry a VIN starting with BA74 and Mk2s BA94, and have the vehicle clarified by owners' clubs before you buy. Proper Mk1s used an Elan-type steering box ratio, a thicker front anti-roll bar and special track-control arms and springs – are they still fitted? On A-frame models check for stress cracks and welding, plus the special Lotus alloy panels are scarce and expensive. The colour of the camboxes is worth remembering: Kingfisher blue signifies the SE tune, red for Cosworth and orange means a rare BRM tune – if genuine, of course!

PRICES

Mk1s are gold dust and pre-aeroflow cars can swap ownership for well over £50,000, £10,000 above a later 'all metal car', and even projects are worth the thick end of £20,000. In contrast, Mk2s are bargains, worth around half the price of a comparable Mk1, because many more were made (4,032), although experts say their values are steadily rising.

VERDICT

You can buy a Cosworth Sierra for less and there are other better fast Fords ... but none hold quite the same appeal as a Lotus Cortina. The Mk1 will always be the king Q classic car, but the Mk2 is better and a lot cheaper.

LOTUS ELISE & EXIGE

(Historics Auctioneers)

With its minimalist nature twinned with advanced racing-principles engineering, light weight and sublime driving qualities, the Elise may well be the best Lotus ever made.

DATES TO REMEMBER

1996   Launched; a mid-engined sports car with a racing-style chassis and MGF 118bhp 16-valve fuel-injected engine.

1998   Higher-powered 187bhp 190 VHPD (Very High Performance Derivative) with race seats and harnesses, roll cage and adjustable suspension introduced.

1999   Elise Sprint, with the 143bhp MGF VVC engine quickly rebadged the 111S, identified by additional rear spoiler and wider rear tyres. Sport 135, of which only fifty were made.

2000   Sport 160: 160bhp from a non-VVC K-Series engine. Harder-core Exige goes on sale resembling a big-winged fixed-head Elise packing a 177bhp engine with option of 190bhp. Special Elises such as the Type 49, Type 79 and GT1 now offered.

2001   S2 has a cleaner look and improvements to chassis.

2004   The 111R now has 1.8-litre Toyota power.

2005   Toyota MR2 power (134bhp) replaces MGF engine. 111R becomes Elise R.

2008   Supercharged 218bhp SC joins range.

DRIVING

The best way to describe the Elise is that it is the embodiment of a modern-day Caterham 7. With a mid-mounted engine for optimum weight distribution, plus light weight and stiffness courtesy of that special alloy superstructure, this Lotus was designed for one thing – the best possible driving experience. All provide shattering performance or amazing economy when not driven at tenth-tenths. Handling is sublime and the ride is typically Lotus supple, but bear in mind that once the sky-high limits are breached, the Elise will bite, especially the S1, and anti-lock brakes were never offered. S1 or S2? As always, the original is the purest in design, but the S2 is every bit as involving but has more forgiving handling.

BUYING TIPS

Whatever Elise floats your boat, the critical thing is to get a good one. Test drive as many as possible, because this car is likely to be so far removed from what you are used to, even a duffer will feel utterly spectacular. This point can't be overstressed, as Elises can be past their best and a bit floppy at around 50,000 miles. Check the chassis (which is difficult to repair properly) for past accident damage and the underside for rippling, again due to previous accidents. The rear sub-frame can corrode, so check its condition along with the underside.

PRICES
S1s are worth the most, but S2 values are fast closing the gap. The very best early Elises trade for over £20,000, maybe more for a special edition and even average ones fall not far short of £15,000, with S2s perhaps worth a few thousand less. Exiges are on another price plane with £50,000 not unknown for an S1.

VERDICT
The Elise is ideal for those who regard Sevens as too prehistoric but want the same panache in a modern package. But it's imperative to buy well and you may have to enlist the help of an Elise expert to do this, but it will be money well spent.

MAZDA MX-5

Huge fun, easy to drive and own with a tremendous choice on offer, right up to brand new. No wonder that the world's best-selling sports car has been lauded 'the new MGB'.

DATES TO REMEMBER
1990   MX-5 goes on sale; 1.6-litre 114bhp.
1991   Officially approved 150bhp Brodie Britain Racing (BBR) turbo conversion with standard ABS offered.
1994   1.8-litre engine replaces 1.6 with 130bhp on tap for the standard car or a higher-spec 1.8iS edition.
1995–7 1.6-litre returns but detuned to 88bhp. Special editions released.
1998   Mk2 dispenses with the Elan-style pop-up headlamps of the original, has a refreshed cabin and more power. 1.8i and higher-spec 1.8i S are available, the latter with power windows and alloy wheels.
1999   Special Edition makes a return, together with 10th Anniversary edition: 600 UK cars.

2001   Known as Mk2.5, ABS, electric windows, central locking are standard and 1.8i S is replaced by the 1.8 Sport.

2005   Mk3 is based upon RX-8 floorpan with 2-litre power and has a more macho look. A powered metal-roofed Roadster arrives soon after.

DRIVING

The MX-5's appeal is so easy to grasp. It's an orthodox sports car based around the old Lotus Elan with similar crisp steering and a click-click gearchange, but twinned with modern user-friendliness and durability, a recipe which has stayed this way for thirty years. The Mk1 is the most classical in character, the Mk2 improved where it mattered, the Mk3 more palatial for touring, if less sporting, but the current car has returned to its roots. One of the MX-5's biggest plusses is that it's a classic that you can use every day (and race at the weekend in specific championships) with impunity just like a VW Golf diesel, and it's as easy to run.

BUYING TIPS

With thirty years of models and goodness knows how many special editions, you need to have a clear vision of what MX-5 you want. Each generation enjoys its own fanbase and it's worth sampling each so you can work out which you prefer. Rust can be problem on Mk1/Mk2s, terminally so if the sills, floor, jacking points and chassis rails are shot. The Mk2 is even more rust prone, but any on the Mk3 will be cosmetic – although check by the windscreen. The mechanics are sturdy, although seized rear callipers are common on all (Mk2s use different systems) and broken springs are not unknown either. There's a plethora of MX-5s specialists around to look after cars and the owners' clubs are really helpful. There are even dedicated racing championships for both standard road-legal cars and out-and-out racers.

PRICES

With a production run still alive and thriving, prices are naturally all over the place, starting from well under £2,000 for a usable MK1/Mk2 (1.8s and Sports holding the most appeal), rising to over £9,000 for a fine late, well-endowed special-edition Mk3. Being the youngest these are still depreciating, and for this reason there's a great cross-over of prices between the classic and contemporary. Of the raft of limited runs, their added desirability shouldn't influence values significantly unless it's a rare Mk1, such as BBR Turbo, or one of the hot Mk3s.

VERDICT

With a model to suit all needs and still in production, no wonder it's the world's best-selling sports car. If the MX-5 has one flaw, it's perhaps that its sheer popularity means that it lacks the exclusivity of a real classic.

MERCEDES-BENZ W113 'PAGODA'

(Historics Auctioneers)

Suave, sophisticated, sensible and sheer good taste, the Pagoda raises the roof wherever it goes. A good one will last a lifetime and running one is extremely easy.

DATES TO REMEMBER

1963   Replacement for the 190SL, the new W113 SL, commonly known as the Pagoda, is based around the W111 saloon, all with fuel injection. The first is badged the 230SL, fitted with a 150bhp 2,306cc straight-six in manual or auto form.

1967   250SL supersedes the 230SL with larger 2.5-litre engine but still rated at 150bhp. However, this was only intended to be an interim model until the 280SL came along, and as a result is the rarest of all the models with just 5,196 made. Summer sees a raft of passive-safety and detail mods introduced.

1968   Final fling is the awaited 280SL with 2.8 litres for 168bhp with optional five-speed transmission, although this model has the softest suspension of all Pagodas.

DRIVING

A different animal to the 190SL, the Pagoda (so called due to its unique hardtop option design) is best as a tourer where the peerless quality of this traditional Mercedes shines through. A very comfortable sports car but the flip side is slightly soft handling, particularly on the 280SL. Ironically, this is the paciest of the Pagodas (0–60mph in 9 seconds), plus it had the option of a five-speed gearbox, although the majority of all SLs are automatics as it suits the Mercedes' touring nature beautifully – even if the rather odd 'back to front' selector needs some getting used to.

BUYING TIPS

One word sums up the SL – expensive. So anything suspiciously cheap is likely to require big money to make good no matter how presentable it may appear on the surface; one SL specialist quotes £90,000 for a proper restoration. Rust spreads to the floor, inner structure and bulkheads. You must insist upon removing the floorpan covers behind the rear seats. The mechanicals are pretty much bomb-proof although overheating isn't unknown. The automatic gearbox lasts forever, but rear axles whine and cost £1,500–£2,000 to put right. The rest of the running gear is usually worry free if genuine parts, such as dampers, have been used.

PRICES

Prices have levelled off lately but are still expensive, with average cars valued at just below £40,000. The best will come in at least double this, and reckon on £100,000 price tags for concours SLs. The 280SL is the most popular, if for no other reason than more were made, with the 250SL the rarest. But experts advise not to hone in on any particular model and instead place condition and honesty first. Colours and trim can make a difference to the prices (silver is the most desired). Three-quarters of 230SLs wore manual transmissions but only 10 per cent of 280SLs, and non-autos are worth some 10 per cent less as are left-hand-drive variants.

VERDICT

The Pagoda was the SL that famous celebrities drove when new back in the 1960s, and they still make highly cultured classics whatever engine is fitted. What the SL lacks as a pure driver's car it makes up in sheer owner satisfaction.

MERCEDES-BENZ R107 SL

The last of the old-school Mercedes, the R107 SL is a safe, solid and satisfying upper-class sports tourer that's built to last and can even be used as a dependable daily driver.

DATES TO REMEMBER

1971 All-new S-Class-derived R107 SL replaces Pagoda with a production run spanning almost twenty years, making it Mercedes' longest-lived model ever. Launch model in Europe was a 200bhp 3.5-litre V8.

1973 European buyers are now able to opt for a mighty 222bhp 4.5-litre engine, now badged the 450SL.

1974 'Economy' SL has 2.8-litre, six-cylinder, sedate but smooth 185bhp engine.

1977 A 2+2 450 SLC is launched with a stretched floorpan and fixed-head roof.

1980 Major facelift includes the arrival of the 380SL and 500SL, using the all-alloy V8 that was introduced in the SLC.

1986 A minor facelift to the SL brings a front chin spoiler to improve high-speed stability and economy for all models, together with a new four-speed automatic gearbox. The 280SL is replaced by the similar six-cylinder 300SL, and the 420SL displaces the 380SL, while for US buyers there's a new 560SL flagship. Swish new high-tech R129 takes over in 1989.

DRIVING

While much improved over the Pagoda, the R107 SL is still not really a traditional sports car, despite lusty performances from the new V8s and much improved handling care of the new S-Class chassis. Pre-1986 SLs feel more classical, but afterwards, the adoption of a four-speed auto and added power gave the SL more urgency. With such a wide choice of engines, problems with enough power are few, but bear in mind that if you are simply wanting one to cruise around in then a six-cylinder version is perfectly acceptable, with the 190bhp 300SL the nicest. Some specialists, such as SL Shop, have a selection for hire and it's a great way to decide which model suits you the best.

BUYING TIPS

With an estimated 2,000 on our roads there are plenty to choose from, but you need to be selective because there are many sad SLs around, that may look the part but are rust heaps. Cars made after 1976 have improved rustproofing, and those post-1986 have galvanised bodyshells. Aside from what you can see, check the subframe and bulkheads as these are costly to put right – the usual giveaway on the latter is wet footwells. A wonky-handling car is possibly due to incorrect chassis geometry settings or fake/aftermarket wheels being fitted. The SL is an okay car to work on yourself, spares are no problem and the owners' club provides great assistance.

PRICES

If you have the money, it's best to buy from a well-known specialist such as the SL Shop, who reconditions its cars and provides a separate warranty on the vulnerable bulkheads for peace of mind. Top cars, usually post-1986, have been known to exceed £50,000, and realistically you need upwards of £25,000 for a sound, rust-free car as anything cheaper is usually a liability. If you want a more affordable SL, check out the SLC, a fixed-head 2+2 with prices perhaps up to half those of an equivalent SL.

VERDICT

The R107 is the thinking person's sports classic. What it lacks in pure driving thrill it compensates for with ownership satisfaction and ease of running. With its army of specialists there can't be a simpler prestige car to own.

MERCEDES BENZ R129 SL

Stylish, swift and sophisticated, the R129 is fast becoming the SL to have, yet it still offers fantastic value for money and should appreciate strongly in value if you buy well.

DATES TO REMEMBER

1989 Virtually all-new R129 takes over from 107, now based upon the latest E-Class and badged as the 500SL, 300SL and 300SL-24 (24V), all bristling with high-tech sophistication. Top 5-litre V8 packs 326bhp.

1992 V12 6-litre, 394bhp 600SL joins range as flagship but tuned V8 400bhp SL60 from AMG tops it.

1994 Model names are changed by simply reversing their symbols, i.e. 500SL becomes the SL500. New (231bhp) 320 replaces previous 300-24. Mille Miglia special-edition cars are now offered.

1997 Optional panoramic glass roof and a special Sports option becomes available on some SLs.

1998 New-look door mirrors plus colour-coded door handles, a change of leather interior trim and 17in wheels are the headlines, but under the bonnet there's a new 224bhp, 3.2 V6 for the SL320.

2001 Final Edition and Silver Arrows special editions.

DRIVING

As a driver's car, the R129 is in another class to the R107 and is far more sporting and precise, yet still smooth and sophisticated where it matters. Think of a better-packaged roofless S-Class and you've got it – although compared to a Porsche it's still not an out-and-out sports car. The straight-six engine range includes a 231bhp 24V, which while notably zestier is not as smooth as the earlier derivatives. The V12 is not needed, to be honest, as the 500SL is almost every bit as good without the complexity and costs. On the other hand, as an all-rounder the SL320 makes an ideal tourer.

BUYING TIPS

Avoid blinged-up cars (of which there are far too many) and those lacking a strong service history, preferably stamped by main dealers or specialists rather than normal garages. Sadly, the R129 was produced at a time when build quality started to slip and rust may well be an issue at the front bulkheads, floor inner structure, etc., although the majority remain in good shape. Ninety per cent of the running gear holds few worries, the exception being the electronically controlled automatic transmission, which can play up, as can the special rear Adaptive Damping System, and it is very expensive and technical to fix. If the handling feels odd, it points to problems here.

PRICES
Compared to the previous SL, R129s are still as cheap as chips but real bargains may be few. They sell for less than £7,000, but relatively minor repairs – such as to the transmissions or hoods – negate any savings and it's best to spend closer to £15,000 for a good, well-cared-for car. Late top-spec R129s, such as the final editions, can exceed £30,000 with Silver Arrows now matching top R107 values.

VERDICT
The R129 is a superb sports tourer and far more of a driver's car than previous SLs. It can be temptingly affordable, but the downside is steep repair costs, so it's imperative that you buy the best that you can, preferably from a specialist.

MERCEDES BENZ SLK

A cute-looking baby SL, the SLK is a great modern classic combining all that's good about the established SL range but in a more youthful, sportier, cheaper and easier-to-run package.

DATES TO REMEMBER
1996 SLK is based upon the 2.3-litre, four-cylinder, 190bhp C230K (supercharged) saloon and initially comes only with one trim level and standard automatic transmission.

2000 Range is refreshed after new bumper and body-coloured side skirting facelift. SLK200 becomes entry level and SLK320 is added to the range. ESP traction control and six-speed automatic are universally standard.

2001 Flagship AMG 3.2 uses twin-spark-plug engine for 349bhp fed via a special gearbox; only 263 RHD UK cars were offered.

2004 Special editions mop up old cars as during the summer a new (R171) SLK succeeds R170 with a new look, longer wheelbase, seven-speed transmissions, added safety features and new engines.

2005   SLK 280 joins the line-up, with a 231bhp, 3.0-litre V6 engine.

2007   Further facelift for a more refreshed look, with higher equipment levels plus a pokier engine line-up. Model subsequently becomes integral with the SL range.

DRIVING

So long as you don't run away with the idea that the SLK isn't Mercedes' rival to the Mazda MX-5, you'll love one. Rather than being a sports car, it's a sporty roadster possessing great year-round usability and owner satisfaction, and it can be used as a daily driver with impunity. As the SLK is based upon the C-Class saloon, albeit with a shorter platform, it's more agile and shaper, but the ride is still good. Performance ranges from mild to wild. The 2004 makeover results in an altogether superior SLK although the styling, inside and out, is not as distinctive as before.

BUYING TIPS

Be warned, there are a lot of shabby SLKs with only price on their side, but these can turn out to be an expensive mistake if, for instance, the hood system requires attention (see that works properly). The difference in build quality between the two SLK generations is deeply significant. While there are some superb examples of the R170 around, the chances of buying a ropey roadster are much higher because serious corrosion is now a major worry, both cosmetic and structural. Six-speed manual gearboxes can be problematic, while the auto's controlling electrics are known troublemakers, and other electrical issues can plague the car.

PRICES

Expect to pay at least £3,000 for a rot-free R170. Nice R171s carry £4,000 price tags at least, and double this for the very best low-milers or a middling AMG R170 ,although with under 300 in the UK, expect five figures for the best. Second-generation AMG editions cost at least £12,000, making the plain V6s at around £6,000 the most sensible SLKs.

VERDICT

Okay, it may a shrunken, lower-ranking SL, but if you want a classy, easy-going, easy-to-own sportster – as opposed to a proper sports car – but with genuine prestige and panache about it, nothing does it quite as well as the SLK.

MASERATI 3200–4200

With the looks and allure of a Ferrari and an even more illustrious name and pedigree – and yet all for the price of a top-end MGB – the super-classy Maserati 3200 is a bargain supercar.

DATES TO REMEMBER

1988   Launched in collaboration with Ferrari as a coupé, the 3200 uses the 370bhp, V8 twin turbo taken from the Quattroporte saloon via a six-speed manual transmission or the more popular four-speed BTR automatic.

1989   GTA (signifying Automatic) is added to the range. RHD models finally filter through.

2001   Assetto Corsa 3200GT introduced as a special limited variant in manual or automatic form featuring a special handling package. The interior is also special to the car. A soft-top Spyder version, shorter by 22cm, joins the range.

2002   The 4200 takes over, looking similar although the unique 'boomerang' rear lights are ditched in favour of a conventional style. The engine is now a fully fledged Ferrari 4.2-litre, 390bhp V8 with new, now rear-mounted, transmission; manual or the Cambiocorsa electro-hydraulic manual using F1 racing technology. The suspension benefits from selectable suspension control with 'Skyhook' adaptive damping and Maserati Stability Programme (MSP).

DRIVING

You can argue among yourselves whether the Maserati ranks as high as an equivalent Ferrari, but it doesn't trail behind by a mile either. In fact, the Italian compares very well to our Aston Martin DB7 with an equally fine pedigree. Of the two ranges, the later 4200 is notably superior thanks to its wonderful Ferrari engine and the new rear-mounted transmission, which not only improves weight distribution but also quells the trigger-happy tail which blighted the 3200GT. Maserati believes that some two-thirds of buyers opted for the 'Cambiocorsa' automatic gearbox.

BUYING TIPS

Special Maserati specialists exist in the UK, and running one is no dearer than any other supercar, with annual servicing ticketed not much more than £600, plus there's a handful of forums and owners' clubs for general help and support and a social scene. The actual hardware is pretty robust, none more so than the engines, although clutches (at around £2,000+ to renew) and crankshaft thrust washers don't last long – that's why an auto is the wisest choice. Other costly expendables are the drive-by-wire throttle modules. Certain suspension and brake parts are also fearfully expensive – plus some are now unobtainable.

PRICES
These Maseratis are the best bargain supercars on the block, costing less than you can pay for a TR6 or MGB! The best 3200GTs fetch in the region of £20,000 but there are plenty of good alternatives pitched from £13,000+. The 4200 range commands only slightly more, unless it's a Spyder where you can add on average £10,000 more, but even so they offer tremendous value.

VERDICT
This is one of the very best modern classics you can buy, not only for value but also for sheer exclusivity. For many enthusiasts it's the only chance to buy a real Italian supercar, but be aware that some repairs are prohibitive.

MG T AND Y TYPE

(Author)

These lovely MG wartime classic sports cars and saloons were the choice of RAF pilots and officers, proving that speed isn't everything. An ideal vintage classic car.

DATES TO REMEMBER
1936   Morris-powered TA sports launched on a traditional chassis but, for the first time for an MG, hydraulic brakes were fitted.
1937   Y Type (YA) saloon has a chassis later adopted for the MG TD.
1939   Identical looking, the TB features new 1,250cc XPAG engine, coupled to a closer-ratio synchromesh gearbox.
1945   TC boasts a slightly wider body and 12-volt electrics.
1947   Four-seater tourer badged YT launched using twin-carb TC engine.
1949   TD keeps familiar look but with a new stiffer chassis and fully independent front suspension plus rack-and-pinion steering.
1951   TD 11 has 57bhp and special suspension damping.
1952   YB facelift has altered rear wings and smaller 15in wheels. Mechanically, a front anti-roll bar, harder suspension and better brakes were the order of the day.

1953　Fared-in headlamp look for TF which is little more than a TD underneath.

1954　TF1500 has 1.5-litre engine.

DRIVING

Based on the common MG TD chassis, it's little wonder that both drive pretty much the same, enjoying similar sharp handling, although the Y Type saloon is noticeably slower (but easily uprated to T Type tune). The pre-war T Types are really for the diehards because of their rear axle design, although many owners claim these are the best handling of the entire bunch. The TF is the best developed, but if you want something a bit more modern yet with the same style, look for the Naylor, which was marketed by MG specialist Naylor using contemporary Morris Marina/Ital mechanicals. Although a replica it commands quite a following.

BUYING TIPS

Not unexpectedly, rust in the body and chassis is the chief enemy and it's odds-on that past repairs have been carried out; pre-TD chassis are the most robust. Apart from metal decay, wood rot of the timber outer frame is major on the T Types and most of it is hidden from view. XPAG engines are expensive to overhaul as they may require specialist machining to make good. Expect to pay £4,000 for a quality overhaul because it's best to have it done by a renowned MG expert. As the design was carried over to later MGs, new or used spare parts are easily sourced.

PRICES

By and large, the saloons are cheaper than the sports cars, the exception being the rare YB Tourer which commands T Type prices, of which the TF and TA–TC are worth the most – well over £30,000 for the best, but tidy runners are half this. Naylor prices are pitched slightly above TF values, and the best value of the bunch is the TD, which fetches between £18,000 and £25,000. If you're on a tight budget, £10,000 should secure a good, honest Y Type saloon, which just needs some TLC, or an LHD T Type for a bit more.

VERDICT

These quaint and quintessentially British wartime MGs are in a class of their own and surely the best vintage sports cars around in terms of low-cost, easy ownership, backed by simply brilliant specialist and owners' club support.

MGA AND TWINCAM

(Author)

Regarded by many as the best MG sports car ever, the MGA was the bridge between the wartime MGs and contemporary sportsters, and a classic that sells on looks alone.

DATES TO REMEMBER

1955 MGA is replacement for the TF although it used the old chassis, albeit larger and uprated, and running gear apart from new 1,489cc B-Series engine, initially tuned for 68bhp.

1956 Great looking Coupé is introduced to supplement existing hardtop accessory for roadsters.

1958 High-power 108bhp Twin Cam relies on past motorsport experience. Based on a strengthened B-Series block with an aluminium twin-cam head, it was not dissimilar to the Jaguar XK unit, but reliability problems ruined the car's reputation and after just two years it was dropped with just 2,111 examples being sold. Twin Cams run on special wheels housing all-round disc brakes.

1959 1600 MkI, in roadster and coupé forms, replaces 1500 and there's now front disc brakes and a 1,588cc powerplant for 72bhp.

1960 De Luxe uses Twin Cam's chassis and its all-round disc brakes; under sixty made.

1961 MkII in standard or De Luxe has 1,622cc engine yielding 86bhp tied to a raised back-axle ratio.

DRIVING

Being based upon the TF chassis, albeit with a lower centre of gravity, the MGA retains all that was good about the T Type and can be made even better easily enough, which is why they remain popular classic motorsport weapons. As a driver's car, these MGs are a pure delight, but despite their updated styling MGA's are not half as refined as they look and performance is only lively at best but easily updated. Capital A is the Twin Cam which sports an entirely different character.

BUYING TIPS

Look beyond the gloss, as many MGAs aren't as good as they look and you need to crawl underneath for a thorough inspection. Sills and A-posts are rot prone, but happily all panels are available, even if they are costly, as is a full restoration. As the vast majority of MGAs were left-hand drive and converted to UK spec (genuine RHD UK cars start with a 1, while export RHD markets begin with a 2) check the conversion has been done properly. The mechanicals are sturdy and easy to fix, not so the Twin Cam engine which still requires specialist know-how.

PRICES

Projects start from £10,000, with the best busting £30,000. There's little difference in values, say a couple of thousand, between the 1500 and 1600 models. Condition is the real dictator although the rarity of the DeLuxe will mean they hold a premium. Twin Cams are in another price bracket, with projects worth double a normal MGA and top 'twins' selling for £50–60,000. Because the A isn't an easy car to restore correctly, high restoration costs of potentially £50,000 should have you thinking carefully before deciding

VERDICT

A better if less-refined classic than the MGB, the A will appeal to drivers – try both to compare before deciding. So long as you buy a good, sound example, the MGA, for its age, is incredibly easy to run and maintain at home.

MGB

(Author)

An evergreen, ubiquitous British favourite that's good to drive and own. For those embarking on buying their first classic car, nothing makes as much sense as the MGB.

DATES TO REMEMBER

1962   Introduced to replace the MGA, the biggest change was its newfangled monocoque design and a 1.8-litre B-Series engine with overdrive option.

1964   Engine gains five main crankshaft bearings for added strength. Pull door handles are replaced by a more conventional type.

1965   Hatchback 2+2 GT launched, which benefits over the roadster with a front anti-roll bar, stiffer springs, wider tyres and a beefier rear axle.

1969   MkII facelift with 'Ford Mustang' frontal.

1973   GT receives V8, plus uprated front anti-roll bar and springs.

1974   For 1975 US laws dictate raised ride right (1.5 inches), re-cambered springs and dele-tion of anti-roll bars. Externally, heavier rubber bumpers, adding 70lb in weight, replace chrome type. Proper 12-volt electrics.

1975/6 Overdrive becomes standard. Special-edition GT Anniversary is identified by British Racing Green paint with contrasting gold side flashes and gold-coloured V8 wheels.

1977   Suspension rethink involves lower-ratio steering rack and new anti-roll bars.
1980   1,100 LEs (420 Roadsters and 580 GTs), all identified by their metallic paint, front spoiler, unique spoked alloy wheels and side stripes to mark the end of production.

DRIVING

Compared to the MGA, the softer-performing MGB is tilted at touring, plus it's appreciably more refined with a roomier, comfier cockpit. Also the availability of overdrive (don't buy an MGB without it) means quieter cruising. Handling isn't as crisp as the MGA and was ruined for 1974 when the ride height was raised to comply with US laws, although a chassis rework for 1977 returned it almost back to chrome-bumper standards.

BUYING TIPS

The good news is that there is an enormous choice still around, and every part you'll need is available, new or used, and there's fantastic specialist support. The bad news is that there are many MGBs on the market not worth bothering with. They rust just about everywhere and while new bodyshells are available, you must cost up repairs carefully in relation to the car's real-world worth. Rubber-bumper models wear their suspensions out quicker, apparently, and has the ride height been lowered back to 'normal'? And if so, has it been done correctly?

PRICES

Sheer weight in numbers means there's one for any budget, starting from as little as £4,500 for a usable rubber-bumper GT, rising to more than £20,000 for the best chrome-bumper roadster, with very early 'pull handle' variants holding a slight price premium. Rubber-bumper models are gaining a following, especially Anniversary and LE limited editions, but don't pay over the odds for a retro chrome conversion MGB.

VERDICT

The MGB is one of the most commonsensical classics you can own because of the superb owner club and specialist support offered, together with easy resales. You'll never be stuck with a good MGB on your hands.

MGC, BGT V8 AND RV8

(Newspress/MG)

If you want an MGB with extra sting, there are three distinctly diverse bigger-engined versions that appeal to different types of enthusiasts. Common to all is easy ownership.

DATES TO REMEMBER

1967 MGC is introduced to replace the Austin-Healey, in roadster and GT forms with a 3-litre straight-six 145bhp engine and a unique torsion-bar front suspension. Available with manual or automatic transmission.

1968 Revised gearbox ratios and differential gearing.

1973 GT V8 has detuned 137bhp Range Rover engine.

1993 Return of V8, now only in roadster form, called the RV8, complete with restyled body, 185bhp 3.9 fuel-injected V8, five-speed gearbox, fully reworked suspension and luxury trim.

DRIVING

Ever since the MGB was introduced, cries for more power were legion – yet this was never reflected in sales. The MGC was intended to replace the Big Healey but turned out to be somewhat lazier and the heavy engine spoiled the MGB's famed agile handling, although not to the extent widely reported because press cars ran on the wrong tyre pressures. Where the MGC scores today is with its relaxed character, making one a great tourer that works well as an automatic. The BGT V8 had the performance the MGC lacked and certainly, with a lighter engine, handles more like the MGB, but was only available in GT form. The RV8 addressed the shortfalls of the earlier Bs and can be seen as the 'new' modern Healey.

BUYING TIPS

Being basically an MGB, much of the earlier buying advice applies except that parts supply isn't as widespread, especially for the MGC, which uses a different floor design and torsion-bar front suspension. Also, while individual body panels are available, complete bodies for the MGC and RV8 aren't produced. Certain six-cylinder engine parts are becoming scarce but perhaps the MGC's biggest weak spot is the gearbox, which isn't up to the job. The Rover V8 unit is well known and is long-lasting so long as the engine doesn't gum up its hydraulic tappets. As the later British Motor Heritage bodies are protected by modern anti-rust treatments, rotten RV8s are extremely rare. Nevertheless, given their rarity (around 350 UK cars but the total tally is now around 500 thanks to re-imports from Japan), it's surprising how many RV8s languish in a sorry state, especially the cabin. Mechanically, check the gearbox and the limited-slip differential for wear.

PRICES

Three distinctly different variations of the MGB yet there's surprising price parity, with MGCs leading the charge by a small margin from the BGT V8. On both don't expect much change from £30,000 for a very nice one and appreciably more if approaching showroom condition. Good examples hover around £25,000+, which is also the maximum for a RV8, which can start from as little as £15,000 for a run-of-the-mill example or a typical Japanese import. What can affect RV8 saleability is its colour; currently green, blue and red hold the most influence.

VERDICT

To decide which is the Queen B for you, it's best to try them all as they all have their own personalities, and while they share the MGB's ease of running they can be a lot dearer to own and maintain, especially the RV8.

MGF/TF

(Author)

The F-word stands for fun with this MG! This is a serious, great-driving, modern, mid-engined sports car that everyone can afford, plus they are low cost and easy to buy and own.

DATES TO REMEMBER

1995   All-new mid-engined, gas-suspended MGF is launched with a 1.8-litre K-Series engine with 120bhp, or a higher revving 145bhp in VVC (variable valve timing) tune.

1999   The 75 LE commemorates seventy-five years of MG production with black and red paint, leather trim and extra chrome. Late summer, a revised MGF is on sale where a CVT-equipped Steptronic auto joins the range, complete with paddle-shifts.

2001   New top and tail editions: a 1.6-litre entry model and the flagship 160bhp Trophy 160. Last F special is the Freestyle.

2002   F evolves into the TF and while looking similar is virtually new underneath. The gas suspension is ditched for a conventional design and Stepspeed replaces Steptronic auto.

Engine line is now a choice of 1.6-litre (115), 1.8-litre (135) and 1.8 VVC (160). TF Sprint special edition is launched.

2008　After MG-Rover ceases, new Chinese owners relaunch TF as the LE500 Limited Edition.

DRIVING

The first all-new MG for decades yet the MGF was a thoroughly up-to-date design as well as the friendliest ever handling mid-engined sports car. The TF is even better but the trade-off is a disappointingly jarring ride (in contrast to the MGF), so much so that, as a result, a 'comfort' kit was quickly devised. A well-kept F/TF is a joy to drive and none can be called slow, but if there's one snag, it's in the gearing which is a tad too tall for a sports car. On the subject of gears, the two automatic MGFs are an acquired taste as their slow-wittedness dulls the driving fun.

BUYING TIPS

This MG's historic low values sent many to the scrapyard and there are not many really good MGFs left, plus certain parts, such as Hydragas spheres and headlamps, are becoming hard to source. Rust is only terminally bad on neglected cars and panels are available. The K-Series is notorious for head-gasket failure, meaning the majority of cars have been fitted with improved gaskets. Also inspect the coolant pipes underneath. Be very wary of the notoriously unreliable automatics as they can cost thousands to repair.

PRICES

These MGs are still great bargains so you don't buy a shabby one just to save money. Fs can start for pennies but the majority of good worthwhile cars – many still with low mileages – sell within the £3,000–£4,000 bracket with the best, and special editions, double this. It's wise to purchase from an MGF specialist as a number sell fully refurbished cars, sporting a new head gasket and a warranty, which can be almost as good as new.

VERDICT

While they are still cheap, the time to buy a good MGF to keep is now because experts predict that their values will only rise in the forthcoming years. And best of all, with so many around, you can afford to be picky as well.

MG MAGNETTE

(Historics Auctioneers)

If you yearn for a 1950s MG sports car but need more space and practicality, the Magnette is not only the perfect solution but is also an entirely creditable cheaper Jaguar substitute.

DATES TO REMEMBER

1953   ZA Magnette is launched at the Earls Court Motor Show, replacing the Y Type with monocoque construction (MG's first) and a new 60bhp 1.5-litre B-Series engine, telescopic damping and rack-and-pinion steering.

1955   A year of gearing changes. At first, a 4.3:1 axle ratio was used before a lower 4.875:1 final drive was fitted to improve acceleration, although at the expense of cruising. So, from chassis 18101, a 4.55:1 differential together with a 64bhp engine became standard issue.

1956   ZB featured the Varitone version, differing with a wider rear window and distinctive two-tone paintwork option.

1959   New MG Magnette MkIII is incorporated into the newly introduced angular-styled Farina saloon range.

1961   Prompt revisions involve a longer wheelbase and wider track to improve the handling. More power came from an engine enlarged to 1,622cc with the saloon uprated to halfway MGA spec at 68bhp. Known as the Magnette MkIV, it was left unchanged until its passing in 1968.

DRIVING

Poles apart best sums up the two Magnette ranges. The zesty ZA/ZB feels far sportier and can be likened to an MGA for all the family to savour, whereas the later 'Farina' version is little more than a glorified Morris Oxford enjoying a bit more power, space and comfort but similar handling. The ZA/ZB is in another league to the 'Farina' and makes a good, much cheaper alternative to a Jaguar 2.4.

BUYING TIPS

Magnette spares and help aren't as widespread as for other classic MGs (NTG Motor Services of Suffolk is the best known) and the bodyshells rust terribly, with sills and floors the worst areas so expect to see repairs of varying quality. Mechanically, Magnettes use a mix of BMC components, making repairs easy, although the downside is the real possibility that normal Austin/Morris parts have been used, which is fine if total originality isn't wanted. On Farinas the added grip of radial tyres can crack the front chassis' steering-box attachment. The Jag-like interior can cost a similar amount to restore, and trim can be pretty difficult to obtain, particularly outside chrome parts.

PRICES

Farinas are the cheapest by a healthy margin, and solid examples are easy to pick up for around £5,000, with the best only a few thousand more. In contrast, ZA/ZB values have rocketed and £10,000 will at best only buy a tidy example. Magnettes holding the most attraction are valued at twice this and prices are rising, but given the cost of a proper restoration are still good value.

VERDICT

The last true MG saloon can rightly be seen as a 'Beginner's Jaguar' but don't think that the Magnette gives you second best. Farinas have their particular place for their sheer value and a touch of class for so little money.

MG MIDGET (AND AUSTIN-HEALEY SPRITE)

(Historics Auctioneers)

A vastly underrated and undervalued sports car that has real character and provides more smiles per mile than anything else for the money. A superb easy-owning starter classic.

DATES TO REMEMBER

1961   Midget, alongside the facelifted Sprite, introduced using original 'Frogeye' running gear.

1962   Bigger 1,098cc engine ramps power from 46bhp to 55bhp. Front disc brakes are now fitted as standard.

1964   Wind-up windows and an improved, more durable 1,098cc engine is installed.

1966   MkIII sees a 1,275cc, 65bhp detuned Cooper S engine utilised.

1971   As agreement with Healey expires, the Sprite is simply called Austin Sprite until the model is dropped entirely.

1972   Round rear wheel arch Midget surfaces, but the design soon reverts back to the stronger square-cut types.

1974   First major change due to US regs: ride height is raised and big black bumpers are grafted on. Also 1.5-litre Triumph Spitfire engine replaces the Austin unit.

1975   MG's golden jubilee year is honoured with a special edition Jubilee Midget, painted green and sporting wide gold side stripes.

1978   Equipment upgrade means dual-circuit brakes, two-speed wipers and hazard warning lights as standard equipment.

DRIVING

Pure and simple sums up the Sprite and Midget (colloquially known as Spridgets) to a tee. These are rudimentary old-school 1950s sports cars not unlike the Lotus/Caterham Seven and provide similar seat-of-the-pants thrills and, if truth be told, handle better and are more fun than the larger MG sportsters. Performance only became remotely lively, but as compensation the MG's raised ride height for 1975 doesn't impair the car as much as it does the MGB.

BUYING TIPS

Spridgets are equally well served by specialists for parts, and with new bodyshells also available (at around £10,000) you can completely rebuild one, although their low values make this financially senseless. If anything, they suffer from rust to a much greater degree than an MGB. All engines are durable and need only the basic checks although the Triumph unit is rather prone to premature bearing wear. Many Spridgets will have been modified to some degree, such as more power and better handling. In the main this is a good thing, and if done right shouldn't influence values either way.

PRICES

The soaring values of the MkI 'Frogeye' Sprite isn't enhancing the value of the other models, but when it does the MkI Midget (MkII Sprite) will feel it first due to its sheer rarity and closest links to the original. Indeed, early Sprites are commanding the most money and it's predicted that the Austin-Healey badge will be worth slightly more in the future. The very best Midgets (the most desired being the short-lived 'round wheel arch' models) would have to be showroom fresh to warrant over £10,000 and most will sell for nearer half to two-thirds of this.

VERDICT

A pseudo Seven? The Spridget offers that same go-kart-like handling and raw nature, plus you won't find a cheaper sports classic that's as easy or low cost to maintain and is a DIY delight. It's a proper little sports car.

MODERN MGS

If you want a sports MG but need something family sized, practical and super cheap, there's no shortage of modern MG hatchbacks, saloons and estates fitting the bill.

DATES TO REMEMBER

1982 MG Metro launched with special 1,275cc 72bhp engine, special body kit and a unique MG-themed interior.

1983 High-performance 93bhp Turbo tops range. Five-door MG Maestro has 1.6-litre, 104bhp R-Series engine with twin Weber carbs and close-ratio VW five-speed gearbox.

1984 R-Series engine is replaced by improved 2-litre fuel injected O-Series for 115bhp. Montego four-door saloon joins range.

1985 Fast, thrilling but unruly 150bhp Turbo tops Montego range.

1987 Chassis retune for Turbo.

1989 Maestro Turbo introduced, with styling by Tickford.

1998 Rover BRM launched; an MGF VVC-powered Rover 200 that pays homage to Rover's links with the Formula 1 BRM (British Racing Motors) team during the 1960s.

2001 Rover 25/45-based ZR and ZS: 1.4, 1.6 and 1.8 engines plus 2.5 V6 for ZS. Also, there's the ZT, which is Rover 75 derived but with a unique MG interior in saloon or estate style, petrol and BMW turbodiesel powered.

2003 ZT range broadened with MGF engine plus a 150bhp turbo offshoot. 4.6-litre, 255bhp Ford Mustang V8-powered range topper is re-engineered with rear-wheel drive.

2004 Facelift for all models.

DRIVING

All are great in their different ways thanks to sparky engines and well-honed chassis designs. Both the ZR hot hatch and track-developed ZS are nice drivers, while the ZT is both a splendid sports saloon or, in ZT-T form, a modern alternative to a Reliant Scimitar GTE. The Mustang-powered 260 has already rightly gained classic status. However, the biggest surprise lies with the Maestro and Montego Turbos where their 'on-off' turbo punch makes for a heroic drive. The Metro Turbo has a distinct Cooper S character about it.

BUYING TIPS

Rust and poor maintenance are the common concerns and spare parts aren't anywhere near as attainable as traditional MG spares, although everything you need is out there somewhere and these modern MGs enjoy a healthy following and strong owners' club support. ZT260 parts are specific, and there are problems due to the marriage of Rover and Ford hardware and cases of broken suspension springs.

PRICES

Prices are as cheap as they can be. The Z cars, along with non-turbocharged Maestros/Montegos, can be purchased for under £1,000, but it's a different matter when talking Turbos (including the Metro) and the ZT 260 V8, where £10,000 and perhaps more can be the order of the day if good and original. Another car that's gaining in price is the one that started it all – the Rover 200 BRM. A solid future classic yet still yours for around £4,000 upwards. But not for long...

VERDICT

These modern MGs provide a lot of classic car, and great variety, for so little money. All drive and handle well and make ideal starter classics as well as fine daily drivers. The ZT-T is an extremely classy and practical sports holdall.

BMC MINI

(Historics Auctioneers)

So much more than a mere car and more of a national treasure, the Mini just keeps on enthralling enthusiasts after six decades and is as much fun to drive as ever.

DATES TO REMEMBER

1959   Launched as the Austin Seven and Morris Mini-Minor; front-wheel driven on 10in wheels by 848cc power.

1960   Austin Mini Countryman, Morris Mini Traveller and Mini van and pick-up announced.

1961   Hot Cooper joins range with tuned 55bhp, 997cc engine, disc brakes, sports gear shift, etc. Luxury saloon-styled Wolseley Hornet and Riley Elf feature a conventional boot.

1963   Cooper S is launched with 970cc race-bred engine and 1,071cc 70bhp in road trim.

1964   Saloons are changed to Hydrolastic (known as 'wet') suspension. Cooper 1,275cc S arrives which soon becomes the mainstay engine.

1967   MkII Mini identified by larger rear screen, bigger rear lights and better trim.

1969   Range shake-up: Elf, Hornet, Traveller and Countryman dropped as snub-nose Clubman comes on stream. Cooper replaced by 1275 GT Clubman.

1984   12in wheels allow for front disc brakes across the range. Metro engines fitted.

1989   Cooper 1275 reappears albeit as a kit, becoming an official model a year later.

1990   1275c engine rated at 64bhp becomes standardised across all Minis.

1991   Fuel injection fitted to all, first official convertible in 1992.

1997   Mk7 is final revision with extra safety kit, front mounted rad and taller gearing.

DRIVING

The Mini is as cheeky and fun-loving today as ever. Not even a Cooper S can be considered quick, but you don't need to go fast to have fun in one; zipping along country roads or nipping through traffic like no other car is just part of the enjoyment. But if you intend to use a one for longish journeys, it's best to opt for a last-of-the-line Mk7 as they run on the tallest gearing and possess acceptable seating, too.

BUYING TIPS

With so many around you are spoilt for choice, and as a result you should take your time deciding. Cunningly clever counterfeit Coopers have been around for decades and, because of their values, are more a danger than ever. A MkI will have a chassis number C-A2S7, MkII C-A2SB. Seek expert advice from a Mini specialist or owners' club if you feel transgressions have taken place. Minis rust for fun and all should be inspected thoroughly, paying special attention to the rear subframe and surrounding floorpan plus inner and outer sills, floorpans, bulkhead – the lot, with some experts reckoning Rover Minis suffer the most.

PRICES

Prices start in the region of £2,000 for a runner with an MOT, up to £50,000 for a concours Cooper S, with Coopers as a rule £10,000 cheaper. The bargains are the Rover Coopers as a good example can be snared for under £7,000. Booted Hornets and Elfs don't attract great values, unlike the vans and pick-ups, which command Cooper prices, with the 1275GT now gaining a following.

VERDICT

The Mini is one of those rare cars that's both classic and contemporary and there's one to suit every budget. For many, it's a wonderful trip down memory lane, but as a starter car for the young it's déjà vu all over again ...

MINI (BMW)

(Author)

This modern take on an old favourite provides just as much enjoyment. The R50 generation appeals to Mini fans of all ages and they are inexpensive to buy and own.

DATES TO REMEMBER

2001   All-new Mini from BMW manifests itself as a three-door hatch using a 1.6-litre Brazilian Chrysler engine; 90bhp in base One model and 115bhp in Cooper (R52) tune, five-speed transmissions and dedicated option packs such as Chilli.

2002   Supercharged Cooper S (R53) has 163bhp, six-speed gearbox and revised chassis.

2003   Toyota-powered diesel D-4D joins range in One and Cooper guises along with John Cooper Works package on the Cooper S, packing 200bhp and a dedicated option list.

2004   Convertible and general facelift (bumpers, lights, etc). Mechanically the troublesome 'Midland' five-speed gearbox is changed for a superior Gertag unit. Cooper S power is upped to 170bhp, and 210bhp in JCW tune, plus a limited-slip differential becomes an optional extra.

2005   Auto option: CVT constantly variable unit for all bar the Cooper S, which gets its own six-speed self-shifter.

2006   Two-seater GP is Cooper S based but 50kg lighter with JCW underpinnings. Special-edition mainstream models offered.

DRIVING

Although it's hardly mini-sized anymore, the R50 design does retain its much-loved Mini character, and this includes the fun factor where the handling and roadholding is as tenacious as ever but with much more performance on hand. A Mini One is quicker than the original Cooper S while the new Cooper S rockets to 60mph in just over 7 seconds. Refinement and comfort is a world away from the original.

BUYING TIPS

First, decide what Mini works best for you – for many it's the peppy Cooper. The supercharged Cooper S is more specialist and dearer to run and maintain. Genuine John Cooper Works versions are becoming gold dust so beware of fakes and look for the Certificate of Authenticity. While corrosion shouldn't be a big problem, rust occurring on the inner door sill is becoming common.

Mechanically the main Achilles heel concerns the five-speed gearboxes, which are a ticking time bomb unlike the six-speed transmissions. Electrical gremlins include failing speedometer and rev counters, window motors, wiper motors and boot release switchgear.

PRICES
You can pick up an early Mini One or Cooper for as little as £1,000, although expect it to be well used. It's more realistic to view £2,000 as a starting point for a decent model with a service history. The Cooper S enjoys a bit of a price advantage but not as much as you'd imagine, unless it's JCW where trade experts predict this model will soar in value to as high as £9,000 if original.

VERDICT
The new-generation Mini is becoming as a much a cult classic as the original, enjoying a similar fun character, but is much more usable on today's roads. As a starter classic and daily driver they are pretty much unbeatable.

MORRIS MINOR AND DERIVATIVES

(Historics Auctioneers)

One of the most endearing classic cars ever, the Morris Minor appeals to a wide fanbase and is loved for its simple, pragmatic and classless nature.

DATES TO REMEMBER
1948 Original Minor (MM) is launched as a two-door saloon, or a convertible named Tourer.

1952 Series II's main change was the new 803cc, 30bhp A-Series engine.

1953 Estate (Traveller), joins range, its USP being a structural part-timbered estate body grafted onto the saloon's platform.

1956 Minor 1000 denotes that the engine is upped to 948cc.

1957 Upmarket Riley 1.5 and Wolseley 1500 offshoot introduced, both based upon a stretched platform and using a 43bhp 1,489cc B-Series engine, with the Riley sporting MG Magnette power.

1961 Special edition lilac-painted Minor called the Million celebrates a million being produced; only 3,550 were officially made.

1962 Last major change sees a 1,098cc engine with closer-ratio gearbox and larger brakes.

DRIVING

Driving a Morris Minor is a delight, providing more smiles per miles than you could imagine. The real pleasure comes not from their outright speed (indeed, the fastest can just about break our legal limit) but from their ever-eager character emphasised by crisp, predictable handling that teaches novice drivers all about rear-wheel-drive control at walking pace. Indeed, such is the car's popularity with younger motorists that a dedicated owners' club exists. Likewise, you need to take account of the all-drum braking system, but this can be easily upgraded, and many are. More speed, space and comfort are available in the shape of the Wolseley 1500 and the sportier Riley 1.5 – both much overlooked quality-badged classics.

BUYING TIPS

There are not many easier classics to own than a Morris Minor. There are loads of specialists around and the owners' club is second to none, not only for help and spares but also with a social scene so good that many owners run one just for this factor alone. Rust runs wild, but all panels are available and it's an easy car to fix at home – apart from structural woodwork on the Traveller, which demands professional repairs costing up to £3,000. Riley and Wolseley are practically identical in design yet parts and trim are harder to source.

PRICES

Buying a Minor is never a major deal as there are so many around, and prices for a tidy runner start from as little as £2,000 for a saloon. That said, Tourers and Travellers are valued notably higher, but are still attainable for under £4,000. At the top end think in the region of £7,000 and £10,000 respectively. Or, if you have the budget, you can have one of the many Minor specialists, like the Charles Ware Morris Minor Centre, build you a good-as-new one to personal spec, incorporating many of the company's worthwhile upgrades. The Riley 1.5 and Wolseley derivatives are broadly based on Minor saloon values.

VERDICT

There are few classics seen in everyday use as much as a Minor. They're reliable and easy to use, and with a few upgrades make a good alternative to a modern, especially as a general run-about. And owner backup is superb.

MORGAN FOURS

(Author)

A Morgan 4/4 or Plus 4 is by no means a second stringer to the celebrated Plus 8, because they provide just as many vintage thrills, are easier to drive and much cheaper to own.

DATES TO REMEMBER

1936   4/4 is launched.

1950   Plus 4 is introduced using a 2.1-litre Triumph TR engine.

1963   Cortina 1500 engine replaces the earlier, weaker 1340 unit.

1971   Road-going 4/4s are fitted with the Ford Kent 1600GT engine.

1981   Twin Cam (a Fiat 1.6-litre engine) is launched.

1982   4/4 switches to 86bhp Ford Escort XR3 CVH power.

1984   Sportier Plus 4 is re-launched with a Fiat 2.0-litre, twin-cam, fuel-injected engine and five-speed gearbox.

1988   140bhp Rover 2.0-litre M16 engine option.

1990   4/4 is fitted with wire wheels as standard.

1991   Ford's 1600 fuel-injected engine is fitted while the Plus 4 gains the wider chassis fitted to the Plus 8.

1992   M16 Rover engine is replaced with the T16 unit in the Plus 4.

1999   Rack-and-pinion steering is fitted. Four-seater 4/4 is re-launched.

2003   Short-lived Runabout is the new entry-level Morgan with a very basic specification.

2006   Plus 4 is re-launched again; 70th Anniversary Edition announced (4/4). Duratec-powered four-seater is launched.

2008   4/4 Sport replaces mainstream 4/4 and uses the new Ford Sigma engine in 115bhp, 1.6-litre tune.

DRIVING

You may pleasantly discover that you don't want a V8 Plus 8 after all. What they lose in outright acceleration (although the Ford Duratec engine produces as much power as the first Plus 8) they compensate for with better agility and more balanced handling. Essentially, the newer the car, the less rudimentary it will feel, but none are refined – but that's part of the attraction. For those who simply desire a Morgan, a post-1999 version with steering by rack and pinion is the ideal choice, say specialists.

BUYING TIPS

Morgans require expert vetting because the body consists of a mixture of steel and aluminium attached to an ash framework and they decay badly, although replacement panels and frames are all available. Cars built after 1986 are the safest bets, and galvanising didn't become standard until 1997. A good way to determine the state of the structure is to check how much slack is in the door hinge post. The safest way to buy a good Morgan is to use a known specialist, because they can help in deciding what model is right for you and they also hold the best cars.

PRICES

Cheaper than a Plus 8, the older the car, the more it will be worth. Expect to pay £15,000+ for a car in a satisfactory state that doesn't require too much TLC. All things being equal, a Plus 4 will command more money due to its rarity, but 4/4 values are more dictated by their condition and provenance than by the year or engine fitted.

VERDICT

Before you buy a Plus 8, check out the wide range of four-cylinder Morgans as you may find that the smaller-engined variant suits your driving style best. And use the expertise of a Morgan dealer when deciding.

MORGAN PLUS 8 AND ROADSTER

(Historics Auctioneers)

A raw, riotous, retro roaster that provides a shattering driving experience like no other classic. But with so many variations of the Plus 8, you need to select your favourite with care.

DATES TO REMEMBER

1968   Plus 8 replaces the Triumph-engined Plus 4 using the 160bhp Rover 3.5-litre V8.
1972   Moss gearbox substituted by the slick shift Rover 3500S unit.
1976   A slightly wider Plus 8 gains the new Rover SD1 engine and five-speed transmission.
1984   Fuel-injection option hikes power to 190bhp.
1986   Fuel injection is standardised. Galvanised chassis becomes optional.
1990   V8 now 3.9 litres.

1995   Rover's excellent R380 gearbox replaces 3500S unit.

1997   Engine gains 220bhp 4.6-litre option. Other revisions include a redesigned dash, while the doors are lengthened and galvanising of the chassis frame becomes standard.

1999   Rack-and-pinion steering fitted.

2002   Commemorative Le Mans edition marks forty years since the company's major success at La Sarthe; only eighty made.

2003   Anniversary edition honours thirty-five years of Plus 8 production.

2004   Jaguar V6 powered Roadster replaces the legendary Plus 8, but unlike the earlier Plus 8, it is also available as a four-seater.

2008   To commemorate fifty years of the model a special (BMW V8) Plus 8 was issued.

DRIVING

When launched in 1968, the vintage Morgan was as fast to 60mph as many exotic supercars and performance has never been an issue with any model of any age. The original Plus 8s possess the most vintage character but are for diehard purists. For mere mortals, the post-1985 versions are recommended by specialists and are better to live with, not least because of their lighter steering. Don't ignore the Jaguar-powered V6 Roadster replacement because it is just as exhilarating. The Roadster is also generally regarded as a far better tourer than the Plus 8 as well as being far easier and lighter to drive.

BUYING TIPS

Because Morgans are highly specialist hand-built classics that require expert vetting, the safest way to secure a good one is to use a specialist as they hold the best cars plus can help in deciding which Plus 8 is right for you. More than likely, unless you see yourself as a Plus 8 connoisseur a pre-1972 car isn't for you as the gearbox and steering are so heavy to use. Roadsters use Morgan's newer construction techniques, which means Superform aluminium wings, a stainless-steel bulkhead and valances.

PRICES

With more than 700 surviving, you can be choosy, but you'd be pretty lucky to find a remotely half decent buy at under £25,000 and can easily double this, especially if it's concours with special history or one of the rare-1975 Plus 8 Sports Lightweights, of which fewer than twenty were made. Original Plus 8s made up to 1972 hold a significant price advantage, making the later cars the best value.

VERDICT

For the majority of Morgan lovers, only a Plus 8 satisfies, but don't ignore the V6 Roadster which may well suit you better. Many dealers hire cars out, which is worth considering as you have to be in the right mood for a Morgan drive.

PEUGEOT GTIS

(Historics Auctioneers)

Peugeot discovered pocket-rocket science with its range of hot hatchbacks of almost forty years ago and have yet to better them for their great driving qualities and typical Gallic panache.

DATES TO REMEMBER

1983   205 hatchback replaces 104 range.

1984   Legendary three-door GTi introduced with a 105bhp, 1.6-litre, fuel-injected engine with 99lb ft of torque.

1986   1,905cc 1.9 engine option tuned to 130bhp.

1987   Big brother 1.9 309GTi introduced, initially as a three-door only.

1989   Minor refresh with detailed cosmetic changes.

1992   Catalytic converters standardised, dropping power back slightly.

1996   306 GTi replaces 205 range with a new 1,998cc 167bhp petrol engine, six-speed transmission and retuned rear suspension featuring 'passive rear steer'.

DRIVING

Peugeot caused a sensation with the 205GTi and a good well-serviced example running on quality tyres – to make the most of its razor-sharp responses, lack of front-wheel-drive fight and a delightful tactile steering – still mightily impresses, although the GTi can prove a tad too nervous at times. The 1.6 engine is the sweeter, but the 1.9 does have a lot more urge and, with its taller gearing, is less fussy at speed. If anything, the larger 309 has friendlier handling and a more supple ride yet is equally adroit at cornering. The 309 also enjoys power steering whereas a number of 205s don't. The 306 continued the good work in a more refined package yet still entertained just as much thanks to its new passive rear-suspension design.

BUYING TIPS

As these Peugeots were meant to be driven hard, expect to find many thrashed and possibly crashed examples. Totally original cars are rare as most left have been tuned and customised. Build quality was only average at best, meaning the majority will be tired and tatty, displaying worn suspension and brakes. Rust is a big problem, even though the shell is galvanised, and made worse as the GTi places extra stress on the bodyshell. Mechanically, the engines can become rattly and blow head gaskets, and it's vital the cambelt is changed on time to prevent it snapping and wrecking the engine. Transmissions can wilt under hard use.

PRICES

Specimen 205GTis have topped close to £30,000, but this a rare occurrence as the bulk are priced anywhere from £2,500 for a runner up to £15,000 for an exemplary 1.9, but watch out for the reborn GTis being made by Peugeot this year if you've the budget. Unless it's the rare luxury Goodwood special edition, 309s are appreciably cheaper; bank on not much more than £5,000 for the best with later 306s even more penny-priced.

VERDICT

Produced during the era when Peugeot made truly great drivers' cars, the GTi versions never fail to excite, but there are not that many good ones around so you'll need to search hard or buy a project to bring back up to spec.

PORSCHE 911

(Author)

A timeless design that's a living legend and still being produced today, the 911 is the most usable and desirable classic supercar in existence.

DATES TO REMEMBER

1963   Legendary 911 announced with a 130bhp, 2-litre, air-cooled powerplant installed in a layout very similar to the earlier 356 (and VW Beetle).

1965   356-engined 912 introduced.

1966   160bhp 911S joins range, weight distribution is altered.

1969   Wheelbase is lengthened and a lighter engine helps rear weight distribution.

1970   Zinc plating aids rust protection; engine is now 2.2 litres.

1972   Engine up to 2.4 litres. Targa-top option, improved rustproofing.

1973   3.0 RS/RSR Carreras came along.

1974   Turbo (930) joins range as engines are upped to 2.7 litres. Galvanised bodies on all.

1979   Full 3 litres for new 188bhp 911SC.

1982   Convertible range replaces Targa.

1984   Carrera 3.2 joins line-up.

1997   Improved G50 transmission.

1989   Major change: coil springs replace original torsion bar suspension set-up. Carrera 2 has 3.6-litre engine plus there's a four-wheel-drive model (Carrera 4) and Tiptronic (semi-auto) transmission options.

1994   Major restyle for 993, the last of the air-cooled 911s.

1998   996 breaks with 911 tradition with a water-cooled engine.

2004   997 sees a welcome return of the traditional 911 look and 321bhp in Carrera tune (3.8-litre S has 350bhp).

DRIVING

While they possess different characters, all feel like a 911 should. The later the car, the easier they are to drive, as the earliest 911s, with their mischievous tail-happy manners, are a real handful, although they became considerably friendlier during the 1970s. 911s can be hard work to drive really well, but the satisfaction of mastering this rear-engined car are immense. You feel more 'at one' with an early 911, but the Carrera 3.2 is the best true 911 for the first-timer.

BUYING TIPS

According to 911 specialist Autofarm, the secret of buying the perfect Porsche 911 is patience. Decide what car and spec you want and insist on a strong service history. Even before you buy, it's a wise move to join one of the numerous owners' clubs or forums first and enlist the help of a 911 specialist. With six decades of production, choice isn't a worry, but a good number are in poor condition. The G50 gearbox is the strongest of them all and unlikely to give any major problems. When you buy your dream 911, use it, as prolonged inactivity really hurts, especially the engines.

PRICES

Chrome-bumper models are worth the most by a long chalk, so if you're on a tight budget then it's best to buy a nice 996, which is great value if not the most classical of 911s. Typically, a decent 911L will cost £70,000, a Carrera 3.2 or 993 around £50,000, and an SC just over the £30,000 mark.

VERDICT

With prices always rising, the 911 is a classic that you buy with your head as well as your heart. Condition as opposed to spec or year is the key to happy, affordable ownership, which usually runs for a long, long time.

PORSCHE BOXSTER

A Porsche that anyone can afford, the Boxster is a genuine sports car that's not only worthy of the badge but is also one of the company's greatest ever concepts.

DATES TO REMEMBER

1996   Launched, a mid-engine sports car relying on front end of the (911) 996 with an all-new six-cylinder engine displacing 2.5 litres.

1999   New high-performance S sporting 3.2 litres, 246bhp with six speeds and a tighter chassis. The base model is also uprated in spec with a bigger 2.7-litre engine.

2001   A variety of colour and trim packs are released; throttle by wire ECU and PSM traction control are the mechanical revisions.

2003   First facelift involves a revised look and power gains; 228bhp, S boosted to 260bhp with 911 Carrera brakes fitted to S.

2005   New 987 range launched, identified by smoother styling, extra power and kit. Spin-off Cayman coupé is introduced to the Boxster range.

2006   S engine is enlarged to 3.4 litres with the base Boxster stretched to 2.9 litres a few years later. Second generation has sleeker styling and added power with the normal Boxster up to 250bhp.

DRIVING

The Boxster is one of Porsche's best ever cars – and that's saying something. With a flat-six engine, and strong links to the 996-generation Porsche 911 (basically the front chassis and its dash layout), the mid-engined Boxster delivers sublime steering and handling qualities, yet feels like an old-school 911 at the same time but without its tail-happiness. While the base 2.5-litre model is generally regarded as sluggish among Boxster experts, its 204bhp more than suffices, although the S is far superior all round. A good many versions employ Porsche's highly acclaimed Tiptronic semi-auto transmission and even if you're not an automatic fan, try one at least before dismissing the thought.

BUYING TIPS

If you're a DIY enthusiast then this Porsche is not for you as engine access is terrible. Besides, what you want to see is a fully stamped service history instead. Rust shouldn't be a problem unless poor accident repairs have been carried out, so check for both. If the Boxster suffers one major flaw, it's with the transmission's IMS (intermediate shaft) fitted to early cars. Also the 2.5 engine is known for its cylinder liners to fail. Check the Tiptronic for missing gears as a repair can exceed the value of early cars.

PRICES

Bargain Boxsters need a watch because while you find them comfortably under £5,000, most will have been hard used (perhaps as a track-day car) and may need expensive repairs in the future. Spending double this opens up a wider scope of choice and condition, the latter counting more than engine spec: 2.9 standard Boxsters sell for around the same price as a 2006 3.4-litre car, for example.

VERDICT

With their temptingly affordable prices, the dream of owning a Porsche is now a reality. But with expensive repairs always a possibility, you need to buy the best you can rather than hone in on one particular model.

FRONT-ENGINED PORSCHES

A different range of practical performance classic Porsches from the 1970s, but no less satisfying, they make fine GTs and can also be surprisingly economical to own.

DATES TO REMEMBER

1977   924 and 928 launched, the former with a 125bhp 2-litre Audi engine, later a 4.5-litre V8 delivering 240bhp, both with a rear-mounted transaxle.

1979/80 928S joins the range with a 4.7-litre 300bhp engine. 924 gains five-speed gearbox along with 170bhp Turbo model.

1982   944 launched, based around 924 Carrera with a 163bhp 2.5-litre engine.

1984   928 S2 has 310bhp plus a four-speed auto.

1985   220bhp Turbo joins range.

1987   928 S4 replaces S2 with new 5-litre engine. 944S has 16-valve engine.

1989   928 GT SE means 330bhp and tweaked chassis with an electronically controlled diff. S2 944 has 3-litre power. Cabriolet range is introduced.

1982	924 revised with Turbo-like suspension.
1985	924S replaces 924 with a detuned 2.5-litre 944 engine.
1992	968 replaces 944 with new looks and a 240bhp 3-litre engine, six-speed gearbox with Sport trim optional.
1993	928 GTS has 5.4 litres, 345bhp and wider rear wheel arches.

DRIVING

All are real Porsches – even the once-mocked Audi-engined 924 – displaying excellent handling thanks to the rear transmission for near-perfect weight distribution. The 928 is a heroic-performing long-distance GT although 80 per cent are automatics. The smaller 944 is the far sportier drive and a Turbo is more than a match for many 911s. The 968 is even better, yet is a strangely overlooked model, despite having added power and a six-speed transmission over a 944.

BUYING TIPS

The 924 and most 944s can be fixed at home at fairly low cost as certain mechanical parts originate from both the 1302 Beetle and early Golfs. The 928s, however, are the opposite and are still complex pieces of expensive kit with far higher running costs. Although bodies are galvanised, rust is still rampant on neglected models and likely to be expensive to put right. Of all the engines, the 944 is the strongest and safest unit. On the 928 the V8 can drop on its mounts leading to a £1,000 repair, and if the automatic gearbox plays up, it can also wreck the engine. Electrically, there are lots of computers and electronics – the front seats alone on some 928s have sixteen separate motors, for example.

PRICES

Prices are hard to fathom. The once-shunned 924 can now sell for more than an early 928 of equal condition. The baseline for a good front-engined Porsche lies between £10,000 and £15,000 and 968s aren't priced any dearer than a like-for-like 944. As a rule, Turbos and cabriolets hold a price advantage of at least 20 per cent.

VERDICT

This triad of pragmatic Porsches are, in their own individual ways, just as appealing as a 911 and far more versatile. As an all-rounder, the 944 and 968 are the best; the secret of happy ownership is to buy the best you can.

RELIANT SCIMITAR

As prestigious as they are practical, the vastly-underrated Scimitar GTE is a world away from Del Boy's three-wheeler van, being vivid, versatile and has that well-known Royal seal of approval.

DATES TO REMEMBER

1964   First Scimitar (SE4) was a fibreglass-bodied coupé powered by the Ford Zodiac's 2.5-litre, six-cylinder engine.

1968   GTE sports hatch (SE5) launched based on the SE4 coupé but larger with improved chassis.

1971   SE5a sees overdrive made standard, uprated Capri 138bhp V6 that September.

1976   Major change as new longer, wider and more luxurious SE6 is launched boasting a 20-gallon fuel tank along with Girling dual-circuit brakes, a better automatic transmission and optional power steering.

1978   SE6a has chassis, suspension and brake revisions.

1979   GTC is launched, turning the estate into a 2+2 cabriolet along the lines of the defunct Triumph Stag.

1980   New Ford 2.8-litre signals the SE6b.

1986/7 Final Reliant-built car made in 1986, delivered to staunch GTE fan HRH Princess Anne.

DRIVING

In its day the Scimitar GTE was one of the best British cars made. Its superb long-distance touring capabilities are legendary and the practical load bay with split rear seating became a lesson to all. Yet for all its versatile nature, the GTE was also a fine driver's car. The larger, heavier SE6 that followed is a more blunted Scimitar although the power-steering option (which is difficult to retro fit) didn't come soon enough. When Ford's 2.8-litre Cologne V6 replaced the trusty Essex unit in 1980, the resulting SE6b became smoother and more palatial but lost much of its lusty nature. The SE4 was a highly acclaimed sports coupé although lacked the superior handling qualities of the latter GTE chassis, but the convertible GTC took over from where the Triumph Stag left off – with some drivers who have owned both preferring the Reliant interpretation.

BUYING TIPS

The good news is that specialist Graham Walker bought the rights to the car after shutdown and has been producing parts ever since, and along with fellow Scimitar experts QRG

(Queensbury Road Garage) can supply just about anything needed, including turn-key ready-to-enjoy rebuilt cars if you have £30,000+. Scimitars are well made and unless neglected the chassis – galvanised on later cars – should be serviceable if the main rails and outriggers are solid. The fibreglass body can suffer cracks and crazing, however, and the interior trim doesn't stand the test of time too well either.

PRICES

The Scimitar is still one of the best-kept classic car secrets and, with the exception of the Middlebridge models, only the early SE4 and the GTC are likely to exceed four figures. Average-to-good cars change hands for around £5,000 and, in general, the SE5 generations are worth most. It is estimated around 3,000 remain so you can be picky.

VERDICT

Princess Anne still owns one – and what's good enough for Royalty ... Scimitars are a cut above the rest and the GTE remains one of the most affordable prestige classics you can buy, but this situation can't last for much longer.

RENAULT ALPINE/GTA

With its rear-engine configuration, supercar pace and tetchy handling, the hand-built Alpine/GTA is Renault Alpine's answer to the Porsche 911 but with much more exclusivity.

DATES TO REMEMBER

1984   Fibreglass-bodied Alpine GTA launched in France, two years before a UK debut, badged as the Alpine V6 GT (D500), a rear-engined coupé.

1985   GTA Turbo (D501) sports a 200bhp, 2,458cc, turbocharged V6.

1990   Wider-bodied GTA Le Mans (D502) replaces both UK models. Only thirty-five right-hand-drive models are made, all in metallic burgundy. Standard equipment includes anti-lock brakes and leather trim.

1992 A610 is the final incarnation, identified by its by pop-up headlamps. Underneath the car is beefed up with power-assisted steering now standard along with anti-lock brakes. The new 3-litre powerplant packs 250bhp for 165mph. Last Alpines produced in 1995 after just sixty-seven right-hand-drive A610s have been made.

DRIVING

As a rarer alternative to a 911 or a Lotus Esprit, Alpines are no poor substitutes. There's ample performance from the excellent Renault V6 – scintillating in A610 tune – and the handling is not unlike that of the 911. Some experts believe that while slower, the standard non-turbo GTA is a better car as it boasts better weight distribution for improved handling and the standard engine has a smoother power delivery, although you need to have your wits about you as common to the design is the tendency to wander and be blown about at speed by crosswinds. As a tourer, the Alpine fares better than a 911 and the interior on later cars is pretty opulent.

BUYING TIPS

There's a smattering of Alpine specialists in the UK and the Renault Alpine Owners' Club (RAOC) is on the ball, but these specialist cars are harder to maintain than a Porsche or Lotus, and some parts are obsolete. The body is complex in make-up with the panels bonded to the chassis. Rot is therefore a major problem, mainly around the sills, suspension-points and cross members, but the fibreglass body is of better quality than a similar Lotus. The V6 is tough apart from head gaskets. On the test drive, any wayward feelings are probably due to odd or old tyres, incorrect chassis geometry (common) or a damaged chassis. Electrics are another source of trouble.

PRICES

The Alpine is one of the cheapest supercars you can lay your hands on. Considering its exclusivity, the prices asked are criminally low, starting from around £5,000 for a tired but basically sound GTA, rising to £25,000+ for an A1 A610. Projects look cheap at only a few thousand pounds, but the cost of many repairs, let alone a major restoration, makes the prospect quite unfeasible.

VERDICT

The GTA and the A610 are tailor made for modern classic car enthusiasts who want something different from the herd. They drive great, look the business and their values can only go one way. But take care when buying.

RENAULT 5 GORDINI AND GT TURBO

Renault was one of the pioneers of the pocket-rocket hatchback during the 1980s and the simplistic fast Fives were the most exhilarating modern classics of their era.

DATES TO REMEMBER

1976   First performance 5 used the famous Gordini name with a 93bhp tune of the 1,397cc engine with a five-speed transmission. Externally the Gordini has distinctive striping and alloy wheels.

1980   5 Turbo launched; an extreme wide-bodied, road-going, albeit two-seater, Renault 5 Gordini, made for motor sport in mind.

1982   Gordini now turbocharged for 110bhp.

1985   Evolution 5GT Turbo is based on new 'Superfive' model and the turbo wick is turned up to 118bhp. Externally there's a subtle body kit, side graphics, new alloy wheels and a revamped interior.

DRIVING

The French Mini Cooper, Gordinis are also light in weight to make the most of their pretty modest power outputs, and their typical Gallic *joie de vivre* all makes a thoroughly entertaining drive. Ignoring the hybrid mid-engined 5 Turbo, which is a different car altogether, the top of the triad of fast Fives is the GT Turbo, which is a breathtaking pocket rocket. This is not simply for its old-school sledgehammer turbo wallop but also because of its superlative handling and roadholding which match that of the Peugeot 205 GTi – and that's saying something – although perhaps not quite with the same finesse.

BUYING TIPS

Fast Fives are thin on the ground. The Renault Turbo Owners' Club (www.rtoc.org) is a good place to start as it will know of any cars up for sale, plus it can put you right because a car may have been re-shelled due to crash damage and Gordinis and GT Turbos use a specially stiffened body. Build quality was never especially good so check for rust everywhere, especially floor, inner wings, windscreen surrounds, jacking points and also bumper mounts. Mechanically, expect wear as these cars will have probably been thrashed to death. Check for excessive smoking and see that the turbo provides a spread of power without undue noise or smoke. Fuelling and poor hot starting were always problems from new on the GT Turbo and a well-worn one will feel loose and crashy. Trim stamina is poor and electrics frequently play up.

PRICES
Leaving out the 5 Turbo, which can sell for up to six figures, there's fair price parity between the Gordinis and the later GT Turbo, although the latter will always fetch a premium of up to £1,000. Something worth owning will cost £5,000 and the best are between £8,000 and £9,000, perhaps a tad more if the car is completely original, which is a real rarity, as is the special edition 1990 GT Turbo Raider.

VERDICT
Now is a good time to buy a rapid Renault while prices are very reasonable, and bear in mind that you can also buy the larger R9 or R11 Turbo family saloons, which enjoy the same basic engine, albeit lesser tuned, for buttons.

ROLLS-ROYCE SILVER CLOUD AND BENTLEY S SERIES

This old-school Rolls, the last of the traditionally built models, will have you on cloud nine with its graceful style, old-world craftsmanship and sheer class.

DATES TO REMEMBER
1955   The Silver Cloud (and the Bentley S1) replaces Dawn and R-Type, still retaining a separate chassis and the old B60 4.8-litre engine, albeit rated at 175bhp. Electrically controlled dampers are standard fitting.

1956   Power steering and air conditioning are placed on the options list.

1957   A variety of body styles are offered , such as a two-door Continental, convertibles and a longer-wheelbase saloon.

1959   Silver Cloud II (and Bentley S2) take over with the chief change being Rolls' all new 6,230cc V8.

1962   Cloud III/S3 is identified by new quad headlamp design. The V8 gains more power, up
        from 185bhp to 200bhp.
1965   New all-monocoque Shadow replaces Cloud, although the design survived as the Phantom
        limousine until fairly recently.

DRIVING

You can't really compare Clouds to the later Shadows, but the uncanny smoothness and silence
of the Cloud still astonishes nearly seventy years on. As a majestic cruiser the Cloud is in its
element, and the real driving pleasure comes from adopting a relaxed attitude making due
allowances for the finger-light, feel-less power steering (the non-assisted models are too heavy
and truck-like to drive for today's owners) and the all-round drum brakes. While the V8 is
appreciably the swifter, the quirky 'overhead inlet/side exhaust-valved' straight-six engine is
the smoother and is super silent. Comfort is second to none and a bench-seated model provides
roomy accommodation for six.

BUYING TIPS

Despite their age, Silver Clouds, and the equivalent Bentleys, are surprisingly easy to maintain,
either at home or via a widespread network of specialists. Parts supply is not a problem as even
the factory can be of assistance and there's also dedicated Rolls salvage experts. 'Horse shoe' rust
at the rear of the chassis must be gauged as it's so expensive to repair. The sheer weight of the car
takes its toll on the suspension and steering, the latter costing up to £1,500 to properly overhaul.
The straight-six engine can last forever, but very early V8s were known to have been troublesome
although would have been dealt with by now.

PRICES

Prices are not yet in the clouds – for standard steel saloons, at any rate – and nice but not concours
cars can exchange hands for less than £50,000. Special-bodied models such as the delectable
dropheads and the Phantom limousine can nudge up to £200,000. It's essential to buy the best
you can, even if it means busting the budget, because restoration costs are prohibitive and good
cars will always appreciate in value. It's not unknown for Bentley models to have been 'Rollerised'
so check the car's history, V5c ownership document and signs of original Bentley markings – an
owners' club can help here.

VERDICT

Clouds are sky high in desirability and always will be. They offer 1950s dignity and decorum, and
some marque oracles regard them as the finest cars Rolls-Royce has ever made. And if you buy a
good one, you may well agree.

ROLLS-ROYCE SILVER SHADOW AND DERIVATIVES

(Historics Auctioneers)

Dubbed the best car in the world, the Shadow has shaken off its used-car trader 'Roller' image and finally emerged as the classy cultured classic it has always been.

DATES TO REMEMBER

1965   Launched as the most technically advanced car in the world at the time and the first mono-coque-constructed Rolls-Royce.

1967   After a two-door coupé followed in 1966, a convertible followed with a power hood.

1969   New three-speed automatic gearbox, longer-wheelbase saloon, identified by its vinyl roof.

1971   Engine's size upped to 6,750cc. Two-door range restyled and rebranded as Corniche.

1972   Steering ratio changed again along with chassis retune to accept radial tyres.

1975   Spin-off Camargue coupé, styled by Italian Pininfarina, launched with more power and new dual-zone air-conditioning system.

1977   Silver Shadow II (Bentley T2) features rack-and-pinion steering, new dash plus rubber bumpers incorporating a front spoiler. Corniche was similarly revised.

1979   To ease production of the replacement, Silver Spirit, Shadow gains its new rear suspension and mineral oil hydraulics – Camargue update follows a year later.

1987   Corniche II gains Silver Spirit's fuel-injected engine.

1989   Corniche III gains airbags and adaptive suspension.

1992   Corniche IV gains new GM four-speed auto and more power.

1995   Corniche S comes with 385bhp Mulsanne Turbo power; only twenty-five made.

DRIVING

The Shadow's character changed during its fifteen-year run, but all enjoy that special sense of occasion. Early pre-1972 cars are more for unhurried wafting around due to their wallowing nature and the car's handling only really improved after 1976, but even so these prestige classics – including the Camargue – are best suited to gliding around in. Performance is adequate but later Camargues and Corniches enjoyed more power, the latter even more so as the mighty Mulsanne Turbo engine was fitted in the Corniche S.

BUYING TIPS

Lots to choose from but a large number languish in a sorry state. Although over half a century old, they are still complex machines to repair and unsuited to DIY maintenance. Rust can be extensive and make some cars unviable to repair, with Corniche and Camargue suffering the worst. Beware of two-tone paintwork along the flanks as it could be masking damage. Being an old-school Roller the mechanicals are built to last, although irregular use can cause engine problems. A proper service of the complex Citroën-derived hydraulic system is essential and can cost around £3,000 depending on who does it.

PRICES

Prices follow buying fads with the pre-1970 'Chippendale dashboard' models currently in demand. You find saloons under £15,000 but these are reckoned to be liabilities and it's wiser to see £25,000 as a plimsol line. Due to their rarity (fewer than 2,000 made), Bentleys command a slight price advantage. The Corniche convertible is valued higher than the Camargue, although values are closing and you're looking at £50,000 for good examples of both.

VERDICT

There is a huge difference between a super Shadow and a merely good one and prices will always reflect this, so buy with care from a good specialist. The Camargue is an acquired taste, but with so few made they are assured classic status like any other Rolls-Royce.

ROVER P5

(Author)

Last of the traditional Rovers, the P5 is a fine alternative to an equivalent Jaguar, providing dignity, decorum and discretion and at much lower prices.

DATES TO REMEMBER

1958   P5 3 Litre is Rover's first monocoque-constructed car, replacing the P4 but still using its IOE (part side valve inlet over exhaust) 115bhp 3-litre straight-six, albeit upped to 2,995cc, and the manual transmission has the choice of overdrive.

1961   By now front discs with a servo become standard issue.

1962 MkIIA has new high-performance (Weslake) cylinder head for 121bhp. Much-loved Coupé body option surfaces.

1963 MkIIB has lighter steering.

1964 MkIIC brings power steering and two-speed wipers as standard.

1965 MkIII features better seats and interior trim. Power increased to 134bhp.

1967 P5B automatic is the biggest change to the P5, now powered by the legendary Buick/Rover V8 engine. Visual changes include Rostyle wheels, side indicators and recessed front fog lights for saloon and Coupé.

1980 Removed from Government service.

DRIVING

The P5 (3.5 Litre) may be not as sporty or as fast as a rival Jaguar but the numerous compensations include superior interior space, greater comfort and a more solid feel. The original 3 Litre is much more sedate than the vivid V8 although its engine is notably the smoother. The P5's handling isn't in the same league as the Jaguar. Rather, you gain more satisfaction with this Rover by letting it glide serenely along and simply enjoying the experience.

BUYING TIPS

Post-war Rovers have been overlooked and rather neglected by enthusiasts, meaning spare parts aren't so prevalent as they are for Jaguars, although much of what you need is around if you look hard enough and there are numerous Rover specialists around. There are a good number of shared parts between the P4 and P5, as well as early Land Rovers. Rust is a real problem, especially at the rear, as a restoration costs as much as a Jaguar but without the resultant residual value benefits.

PRICES

The overall standard of cars is average at best and these are priced around £5,000, but the best P5B Coupés can fetch as much as three times this with £20,000 for something special becoming quite common. As a rule, equivalent 3.5 saloons are worth some £4,000 less, as are all 3 Litre cars and while the bargain buys are dwindling, compared to a Jaguar of the same era they still represent exceptional value for money but only if they are structurally sound.

VERDICT

The P5 remains one of Rover's best ever cars and is still highly revered by owners of all ages. The P5B Coupé is the model the majority go for, but the more sober-suited saloon and 3 Litre are also worth owning. Just try one.

ROVER P6

(Historics Auctioneers)

The first Car of the Year winner, the innovative P6 2000 is the last of the real Rovers and remains a bargain-priced classic, which can double up as a feasible daily driver.

DATES TO REMEMBER

1963   All-new P6 launched featuring an innovative skeleton body and chassis frame with bolt-on panels. Available only with a 1,978cc, 90bhp, four-pot engine and advanced running gear such as De Dion rear suspension.

1966   TC (stands for twin carb and raises power from 90bhp to 114bhp) and automatic models join range.

1968   Flagship 3500 features Rover's new 144bhp 3.5-litre V8 but as an automatic only.

1970   First facelift sees new frontal styling.

1971   3500S is a manual transmission 3500 V8 with sporty touches although automatic is still an option.

1973   Engine is stretched to 2.2 litres to become the 2200 range.

1977   Production ceases as Rover expands SD1 range, although some cars hang around in dealerships for a good while afterwards.

DRIVING

The BMW-beating P6 was so advanced for its time that a good one still acquits itself well today. Handling and comfort, thanks to its radical suspension design, was the Rover's forte, and while the P6 does roll noticeably during hearty cornering the roadholding is quite tenacious. Performance from the V8 and TC models is good; in contrast, the normal SC (single carb) models feel sluggish, with the 2000 automatic being positively lethargic, but all models cruise well in commendable comfort. The P6 is at its best on long journeys as the heaviness of the steering, the less-than-slick gearchange along with the lack of torque from the four-cylinder engines can make town driving a bit of a chore.

BUYING TIPS

As the P6 has been another overlooked Rover classic, spare parts and specialist supply have suffered and it's mostly used parts that are available. Ely Service (elyservice.co.uk), JR Wadhams (jrwadhams.co.uk), Rimmer Bros and MGBD Parts (roverp6parts.com) will help, as will the P6

Rover Owners' Club (p6roc.co.uk) and Rover P6 Club (p6club.com). The state of the skeleton structure is the real deal maker or breaker, and you need to remove the rear seat for a thorough inspection. The engines are durable but quite involved for DIY work, as are the rear brakes and the associated De Dion rear suspension – both may be neglected as a result. Good second-hand interiors are getting scarce, and they don't age that well.

PRICES

The best way to sum up the P6 is that it offers prestige for peanuts – only the 3500 range is likely to exceed £10,000 if in A1 condition, and it's more than likely that you will pick up any perfectly sound P6 for around £6,000, with rattly cars half this. Projects cost pennies, but given the scarcity of parts and rust problems, buying one will be a labour of love rather than a money maker.

VERDICT

The P6 is a cultured if cramped quality saloon that makes a great bargain-priced classic that enjoys a far better reputation than the SD1 that replaced it. My choice would be a TC or 3500, although condition counts the most.

ROVER SD1

(Historics Auctioneers)

The Ferrari Daytona-nosed SD1 is the last independently made Rover and it gained a questionable reputation. A good one is a great car to drive as well as being very practical.

DATES TO REMEMBER

1976 Launched that summer to replace the P6, which ran for another year. The SD1 was a V8-powered five-door hatchback saloon with only one trim level.

1977 SD1 was complemented by the six-cylinder, 123bhp 2300 and 136bhp 2600 models, the badging denoting their engine sizes.

1979 V8-S is identified by its unique gold alloy wheels.

1982 Facelift sees enlarged rear window and new dashboard among other changes. New engine additions to the range included a 2-litre (petrol 2000) and a 2.4-litre turbodiesel, which was also used in the Range Rover, while model trim levels were bolstered by a 2600SE and V8 Vitesse.

1985   Brutal special Lotus-developed 'Twin-Plenum' 190bhp Vitesse and luxury Vanden Plas models are launched.

DRIVING

Although a much simpler car than the trailblazing P6 it replaced, the SD1 is a car that in its day was equal to its German rivals in all departments, including driving pleasure. The handling, once you become accustomed to the hyper-sensitive power steering, is excellent – witness the SD1's success in motorsport – and the V8 provides both strong performance that's scintillating in 190bhp Vitesse tune and surprising economy thanks to tall gearing. As a practical prestigious classic, the hatchback Rover has much to offer, and as a sports saloon, it is one of the best. The normal V8 range is a bit of a wolf in sheep's clothing, but the winged 190bhp Vitesse has the feel and flavour of an Aston about it.

BUYING TIPS

If only the Rover wasn't such a dog in its day then the SD1 would be one of the best modern classics on the block – as many satisfied owners will testify. Because values have bottomed out for yonks, cheapskate ownership is rife, but spares supply is amazingly good from Rimmer Bros, who produce a dedicated parts catalogue. Rust is a worry and the six-cylinder, Triumph-based engines are an absolute nightmare, as are the electrics and trim. The Boge Nivomat self-levelling rear suspension is usually ditched once it fails due to the cost of repairs.

PRICES

You get what you pay for with this classic. It starts from £1,000 or so for a ragged runner, rising to five figures for a mint Vitesse or VDP. Anything in between is dependent on condition, although original 1976 cars are starting to find a following.

VERDICT

Every dog has its day and the SD1 deserves to have one. A great design, let down by poor build, a good Rover SD1 is a joy to drive and own and few classics are as versatile. Condition is the key factor, but be very wary of a 2300/2600 no matter how good unless you know the engine is sound.

SUNBEAM ALPINE AND TIGER

(Historics Auctioneers)

With its 1950s finned styling, Sunbeam's Alpine is probably Britain's most overlooked classic sports car, even though it has just as much to offer as any rival. The Tiger is the ultimate Q car.

DATES TO REMEMBER

1959 Sunbeam Alpine, based upon a Hillman Husky van-derived chassis, goes on sale, with a 1,494cc Rapier engine, four-speed manual gearbox and (optional) overdrive.

1961 SII benefits from a 1,592cc, 80bhp engine and uprated rear suspension.

1963 Alpine SIII sees suspension revised including a stouter front anti-roll bar and telescopic rear dampers. Alpine GT is hard-topped version.

1964 V8 Tiger launched in US has Ford 4.2-litre engine rated at 164bhp. Alpine IV is smoother looking, thanks to reduced rear fins.

1965 RHD Tiger goes on sale in the UK in the spring. Alpine V is now is now 1,725cc.

1967 A MkII Tiger features a Ford 200bhp 4.7-litre V8.

DRIVING

The Alpine is a smoother, softer, slower alternative to an MGB or TR Triumph and more tailored for touring, although the Sunbeam can be easily tuned to become sportier. In fact, a good many have been fitted with the Rapier H120 engine by owners, although opinions are split on this racy powerplant for road use and some Alpine owners claim that the 1600 SII model is the nicest and sweetest performer if not the most rapid. Where the Sunbeam really shines is with its restful ride and comfy seating. The Tiger addressed any performance issues and was quite a Q car in its day, and although it doesn't handle much better than the Alpine it's based upon, that lusty V8 is a joy and adds a lovely soundtrack to the bargain.

BUYING TIPS

Alpines and Tigers are well supported by their relevant owners' clubs, so spares and advice aren't a major problem, although running one isn't as easy as an MGB. Contrary to popular belief, the Tiger's shell is not unique and both rust badly at the sills, floor, cruciform, bulkheads and suspension points. Most Tigers will be original (although later V8s may be fitted to ease parts availability), unlike Alpines that may have been repaired with plain Hillman Minx saloon parts due to their inherently low values. For example, the engine's camshaft was special to the Alpine, but one expert claims over 90 per cent will now use a Rapier alternative.

PRICES

Alpine prices have risen lately, and while still less expensive than an MGB, the gap has closed appreciably and the best can top £20,000. Typically, half of this will secure a good, sound example. Tigers are far pricier and £60,000 is by no means uncommon for a concours car, with merely average examples still valued at close to £30,000, and their prices, which already exceed those on the legendary Big Healey, can only rise over the years.

VERDICT

These Rootes roadsters make a pleasant change to the usual MG and Triumph offerings and are certainly nicer tourers, if not such a sporty drive. Early Alpines are the most sought-after, but 1963 cars are much better to drive.

SUBARU IMPREZA TURBO

The Japanese 'Cosworth Sierra', Subaru's Impreza Turbo is arguably even more accomplished, very reliable and amazingly usable and yet prices remain at bargain levels.

DATES TO REMEMBER

1994   Two years after its launch the first Turbos arrive in the UK; a four-wheel-drive saloon or five-door hatcheck with a 2-litre, flat-four, turbocharged engine rated at 218bhp.

1995   The first special edition, the Series McRae edition, is launched to celebrate the car's victory in the RAC Rally with a build of 200.

1997   Models have revised styling, refreshed interior and a torquier engine. Catalunya is another special edition in black paint livery with gold five-spoke alloys.

1998   Terzo: another limited run (333) the car came in blue with gold alloys. The most exclusive Impreza of them all is the 2.2-litre 276bhp Prodrive-modified 22B. Just sixteen were sold in the UK.

1999   Big revision with new looks plus a new engine and revised suspension and brakes. Final fling for the Mk1 was the RB5 limited edition. Named in honour of Works driver, the late Richard Burns.

2000   Second-generation Impreza Turbo WRX STi has debatable 'bug-eyed' look but is mechanically similar and ran until 2007.

DRIVING

The great thing about the Impreza Turbo, apart from the superglue all-wheel-drive grip and an undeniable feeling of invincibility on all surfaces, is that it has a lovely classic rawness about it, not least the gruff gravelly sounding 'boxer' engine that's not dissimilar to a Porsche 911. It packs a similar punch (0–60mph in 6 seconds) too, with a gushing yet linear power delivery, even if a lack of low-rev torque means you have to work this engine to get the best from it – but that's hardly a hardship. Available in saloon and hatchback styles, the Subaru is as practical as a Golf and as usable day in, day out.

BUYING TIPS

There's no shortage of choice, but you need to know what you're buying, as apart from official UK models there are also 'grey imports' from Japan (brought in by independent dealers) which may have a different specification. Also be wary of sporty Imprezas which may not even have four-wheel drive; an owners' club will put you right on both worries and can verify if a particular limited edition isn't a cunning fake. Subarus are trusty but can be really rusty. However, the biggest concern is previous crash damage. By the same token, many are modified, but if done well that's to your benefit if originality isn't a problem.

PRICES

While rivals such as Ford's Cosworths and the Lancia Integrale have soared in value, Imprezas have remained almost unbeatable value in comparison and you can easily buy a standard but solid and sound WRX comfortably under £10,000, although the special editions are a different matter. Best bargains are the second-generation cars, where £3,000 can buy a very nice example that makes a fine and dependable daily driver.

VERDICT

Suburu's Impreza Turbo is one of the best, and certainly one of the wisest, modern classics thanks to their durability and sheer usability. If you've always yearned for a 911 but need something more practical, this brilliant rally legend could be the answer.

TRIUMPH HERALD AND DERIVATIVES

(Historics Auctioneers)

These Triumphs epitomised 'middle England' and as a result, they are always seen as a cut above the rest. There's something for everybody at very good prices.

DATES TO REMEMBER

1959   Herald announced as a two-door saloon or coupé built on a separate chassis with an independent rear suspension and powered by a 948cc engine.

1960   Convertible launched.

1962   Spitfire sports car is based upon a shortened Herald chassis with a 63bhp, 1,147cc engine. Herald-looking Vitesse performance offshoot has a 1.6-litre, 70bhp, six-cylinder engine.

1963   12/50 Herald features a semi-Spitfire tune engine (51bhp), front disc brakes and a folding sunroof as standard.

1965   Mk2 Spitfire has slightly more power (67bhp) and a plusher interior.

1966   Spitfire-based coupé-styled GT6 launched using the 95bhp Triumph 2000 six-cylinder engine, as now does the Vitesse.

1967   Engine is stretched to 1,296cc and 71bhp to create Spitfire Mk3 and the 61bhp 13/60 Herald range.

1968   Vitesse and GT6 gain redesigned rear suspension and 104bhp engine tune.

1970   Spitfire Mk4 enjoys a smoother look with Stag-style tail, new interior and fully revised rear suspension. GT6 also receives similar changes.

1973   Latest Spitfire rear suspension plus brake servo are fitted to GT6 before car is discontinued.

1974   Spitfire engine is stretched to 1.5-litres for 71bhp with trim upgrades.

DRIVING

As they all use a basic Herald chassis there's a fair bit of commonality in how they drive, and common to all is their contentious rear-suspension design, which on the more powerful models needs watching. Modern radial tyres improve things greatly, plus there's a number of well-developed tuning parts available from specialists. The Spitfire is a more stylish and softer alternative to an MG Midget but no less fun and has the benefit of optional overdrive; it's generally accepted that the Mk3 is the best model. The GT6 has been likened to a 'mini E-Type' due to its looks and swift, silky six-pot power – again, overdrive makes the 'super Spitfire' a lovely cruiser. The Vitesse is a hotter Herald that's no dearer to run.

BUYING TIPS

The Triumph marque is one of the best supported by specialists and owners' clubs so parts and help are always at hand. The separate chassis frame ensures straightforward repairs for inevitable rusting, and the bodies can be lifted off to facilitate major jobs or a replacement frame if desired as they are available. Body rot can be substantial, though.

PRICES

In the pecking order, Heralds are the cheapest by a fair stretch followed by the Vitesse, and both remain good value at £5,000 tops for the best saloons, although concours convertibles can be worth twice as much. Spitfires have really taken off of late and five-figure asking prices are becoming the norm for top-flight Mk2s and Mk3s, although the later Mk4 and 1500 versions remain considerably cheaper. GT6s can now match TR6 values and at least £8,000 is required for a remotely sound car.

VERDICT

Final choices boil down to personal preference but I would opt for a Vitesse over a Herald due to its much better performance yet similar running costs. The overlooked GT6 really is almost a mini E-Type in looks and character.

TRIUMPH STAG

The Stag is one of the UK's most popular classics with a great owners' club and specialist backup, both of which have turned this cabrio into a better car now than when it was brand new.

DATES TO REMEMBER

1970   The Triumph 2.5PI-derived Stag 2+2 is finally launched almost two years late. Engine changed from the former straight 2.5-litre six to a dedicated 145bhp 3-litre V8 with a choice of manual or automatic transmissions, hard and soft tops and a wire-wheel option.

1972   Overdrive (on third and top gears) is now standard fitting.

1973   Mk2 is marked out by its matt-black tail panel and sills plus new wheel trims. Previously optional hard top becomes standard. Mechanically, the notoriously fickle V8 gains a modified cooling system.

1975   Alloy wheels, tinted glass, seat-belt warning, hazard flashers and a laminated windscreen all become part of the package for 1976.

DRIVING

Stags are so satisfying. The V8 is a gem providing adequate performance as well as glorious sound, and the Stag is a great hood-down sports tourer for all the family – in contrast, the hard top creates too much wind noise. Automatic transmission suits the car to a tee although a manual overdrive transmission is less fussy at speed and yields better fuel economy. The Stag is no sports car like the TR6 yet it does handle with more security. Due to the engine's infamous reliability reputation, a fair number received alien power units during the 1970s/80s with the 3.5-litre Rover V8 being the most popular fitment. Apart from being more trustworthy, it's also more powerful, but the downside is the installation upsets the Stag's weight distribution and so the handling suffers accordingly unless the suspension is revised – but many aren't.

BUYING TIPS

Few classics are as well supported as a Stag and ownership is no problem, plus there's always a healthy market for good examples. Serious rusting makes some cars uneconomic to restore. The Stag's V8 engine has always been a bane, but development by specialists has cured its ills. Most issues centre around the cooling system and resultant overheating. If considering a Rover V8 transplant Stag, check the workmanship and see that the handling is to your satisfaction.

PRICES

To avoid owning a liability, the budget needs to be at least £8,000 for a scruffy but sound factory-spec Stag and well-kept ones will easily require that much again. Super Stags, from a known specialist, now bust the £20,000 barrier. Rover V8 transplants are falling out of favour and so are the cheapest bets.

VERDICT

Now the Stag has finally shaken off its 'snag' nickname, this Triumph has become a cut-price substitute for a Mercedes SL with as much style and class. With one of the longest-serving owners' clubs, the social scene is first rate too.

TRIUMPH TR2-6

(Histories Auctioneers)

Beefy traditional British roadsters that typified the sports-car scene during the 1950s and '60s, TRs are super classics that are backed by fantastic specialist and club support.

DATES TO REMEMBER

1953   TR2 launched based on a revamped pre-war Standard Flying Nine chassis with a Standard Vanguard four-cylinder engine.

1954   Due to the car's doors snagging high kerbs by late 1954, they were shortened and a sill inserted to take up the gap.

1955   TR3's notable styling revision was its 'egg-crate' grille.

1956   Standard-issue front disc brakes.

1957   TR3A, recognised by a full-width grille and has an improved cockpit.

1961   TR4 is a complete rethink and restyle. The larger chassis is improved by rack-and-pinion steering and servo-assisted brakes, while the interior enjoys proper ventilation and wind-up windows.

1965   TR4A brings new independent rear suspension (taken from Triumph 2000 saloon), woodgrain dash and styling improvements.

1967   TR5PI is essentially a TR4 but with a 150bhp, fuel-injected, 2.5-litre, six-cylinder engine.

1969   TR6 PI replacement has clever modernised top-and-tail re-body.

1973   Engine is detuned to 125bhp but overdrive becomes standard.

DRIVING

There's a certain rugged rawness about all Triumph TRs that's not dissimilar to a Morgan. The TR2 and TR3 are the most spry and sporty as they are the lightest, while the TR4 has a character all of its own, being the bridge between the rudimentary models of the 1950s and the softer 1960s alternatives. Opinions are split over the TR4 and 4A; the latter's independent suspension improves grip and ride – but many prefer the tactile feel of the earlier car. The six-cylinder TR5 and TR6 have a lusty performance about them. Don't, like many enthusiasts do, get too hung up about the '150bhp' engine tune, as in real-world driving there's little difference between the pair.

BUYING TIPS

Finding totally standard TRs is proving increasingly hard, although accepted improvements make them all nicer and safer. As most went to the US, RHD converts are rife but are fine if done properly. Rusty chassis are commonplace and a good test is to jack up the car and watch for the door gaps to alter. All engines are rugged but suffer from the usual Triumph foible of excessive crankshaft end float. The Lucas fuel injection was once avoided like the plague and many were converted to carburettors, but a good specialist can make it trustworthy and perform better than when new.

PRICES

Apart from the limited-run TR5PI, of which less than 3,000 were made, there's not much in it between the ranges, with the TR6 lagging behind. Expect to pay in the region of £30,000 for the best four-cylinder TRs, with the TR3 holding a very slight price advantage. Merely good TRs sit in the low-to-mid £20,000 bracket, but a TR6 may be £5–£10,000 cheaper.

VERDICT

Charming and quintessentially British sports cars that are all easy and enjoyable to own and maintain, but you need to determine which era suits you best. Out of them all, the TR4 is increasingly seen as the best all-rounder.

TRIUMPH DOLOMITES

(Historics Auctioneers)

Triumph's mid-sized saloons remain one of the best-value prestige family classics around and are ideal for the impecunious enthusiast craving an easy-owning sporting saloon which has a touch of class about it.

DATES TO REMEMBER

1965   1300 launched as front-wheel-drive, four-door saloon with a 2000-style look and a similarly themed interior.

1967   1300TC added to range using a 75bhp Spitfire-tune engine plus brake servo.

1970   Range shake-up. New Toledo is launched to replace Herald using a new (two-door) 1300 body and a simpler rear-wheel-drive configuration. Old 1300 morphs into a larger, longer-tailed 1500.

1972   Dolomite 1850 introduced relying on the 1500 bodyshell using a new OHC engine first developed for Saab but re-engineered for real-wheel drive.

1973   Dolomite Sprint has special 127bhp, 2-litre, 16-valve, single-OHC engine. Toledo gains four-door option while FWD 1500 evolves into rear-wheel drive, like the Dolomite 1850, but with the twin-carb Spitfire engine and badged the 1500TC.

1976   Dolomite becomes the new generic saloon name with overdrive option for 1500TC.

DRIVING

All saloons are solid, capable drivers, but they have split personalities because of their differing transmission formats; the Dolomite Sprint is the performance pick due to its hard-charging if rather coarse 16-valve engine, although the 1850 Dolomite is pretty lively, and one of the benefits of the rear-wheel-drive models is the option of overdrive for less-fussy cruising. Common to all saloons are their rich and sumptuous, if cramped, interiors.

BUYING TIPS

Parts supply isn't bad but not up to other Triumph classics, with the saloons suffering the most, compounded by too many lower-rank models being sacrificed for their bits to save a sad Sprint. Rust attacks all the usual places. The 'half Stag' four-cylinder utilised by the Dolomite 1850 and Sprint suffers serious issues with similar overheating problems, and the cylinder heads can prove virtually impossible to remove at the kerbside if they become rusted on – as many are. Aside from the gearboxes, the rest of the running gear holds few worries although FWD parts are becoming scarce.

PRICES

With the recent exception of the Sprint, saloons sell for a pittance and £4,000 is ample for the best, irrespective of the model, with average alternatives half the price. Sprints, on the other hand, have now realised their rightful classic status and have risen in price sharply, but even so, under £10,000 easily suffices for a very nice original example.

VERDICT

Not the most sought-after Triumphs, but all make excellent starter classics. The saloons have blue-rinsed 'middle England' written all over them while a good Sprint will surely become a sought-after classic in the near future.

TRIUMPH TR7/ TR8

The TR7 was never intended as a direct replacement for the much-loved hairy-chested TR roadsters, yet is still a very likeable sports car that's excellent value for money.

DATES TO REMEMBER

1976   All-new totally modern Triumph sports car is launched to replace the TR6 using a mono-coque construction and principally Dolomite saloon mechanicals.

1977   Normal plain cloth Dolomite seating trim is replaced by a vibrant red or green tartan style.

1978   Production shifts to Canley and these cars are identified by having a garland transfer on the nose. There are several well-known variations and special editions, such as the Premium (black with gold decals); the TR7 Sprint with a Dolomite 16-valve Sprint engine; the Spider, which is black with a hint of red in it (Maraschino) and red stripes; and the Coca Cola cars, which were given away as competition prizes.

1979   Previously optional five-speed manual is now standard. Long-awaited convertible is launched, initially for the US market.

1980   As rag tops arrive in UK showrooms, the US enjoys the long-awaited Rover-powered (135bhp) TR8. It's believed that only twenty official UK models were made.

DRIVING

While it relies largely on Dolomite hardware, the TR7 is a different car entirely (not dissimilar to the Jensen-Healey) and boasts a unique chassis. It still feels too soft and saloon-like when compared to previous harder-core TRs, but the handling is far superior to what came before. The TR7's forte lies in its comfort and refinement, which is most un-TR-like, and the Triumph is a good replacement for both the TR6 and the GT6. Even though the 'half Dolomite Sprint' engine posts 105bhp and performance that's almost as good as an average TR6, it lacks that essential sports-car spirit and sound. There are many TR7s converted to Rover V8 power (indeed, specialist Rimmer Bros has devised a range of kits to enable this). The proper TR8 uses the mildest 135bhp Range Rover unit.

BUYING TIPS

The TR7 is pretty well served for parts. Rimmer Bros, in fact, markets a complete body restoration kit for less than £1,500. Due to low values, many have suffered neglect and as a result rust can be especially bad. It is said that the Speke-built cars used better materials, but actual build quality is reckoned to be the worst of the three sites that made the car.

PRICES

The most-valued TR7s are the official TR8 convertibles (£10,000+), followed by a converted TR7-V8. The ultra-rare 16V Sprints, of which sixty were officially made, are hard to value but fall somewhere between a 2-litre and a home-spun V8, as do the special-edition variants. Anything between £3,000 and £5,000+ secures a very tidy TR7 coupé, with the convertible worth an additional £2,000.

VERDICT

Once the butt of jokes for being a walk on the mild side, this much-maligned sportster is now being seen in an entirely new light. As a matter of fact, a fair number of early TR drivers also now own a TR7 for when the mood takes them.

TVR CHIMAERA AND CERBERA

Big, bold and beefy – and bargains – Chimaera and Cerbera are two certain future modern classics. As top-rank drivers' cars they match any supercar for pure pace and thrills.

DATES TO REMEMBER

1992   New Chimaera debuts. Essentially it's a rebodied Griffith with a slightly softer nature and added room. Power comes from TVR-tuned Rover V8s of 4.0 litres (240bhp) and 4.3 litres (280bhp), while the Griffith chassis has softer springing.

1994   Chimaera 500 has 5-litre 320bhp Rover V8 power. A new Borg Warner T5 gearbox supersedes the Rover unit across the ranges.

1996   Facelift sees a new nose style, colour-coded bumper and longer boot lid. Door opening buttons are moved to the door mirrors. Fixed-head 2+2 Cerbera launched, based upon Chimaera but uses TVR's own AJP engine, originally a 4.2 V8 punching out 350bhp.

1997   4.5-litre 420bhp engine option for Cerbera with standard Hydratrak rear axle. Chimaera receives a mild facelift for 1998 which includes standard power steering.

1999   New entry-level Cerbera utilises new AJP straight-six called Speed Six; 3,996cc, 350bhp.

2001   Chimaera now boasts enclosed headlights a la Griffith. Cerbera seats are now fitted. Cerbera Red Rose option pack consists of a more powerful 4.5-litre engine (440bhp) with bigger brakes plus suspension upgrades to cope.

DRIVING

'Awesome' best describes this pair of TVRs, but even then that's an understatement. Shorn of anti-lock brakes and any driving aids but packed with pure power, if ever there was a modern interpretation of the hairy-chested Austin-Healey here they are. Handling ranks as some of the best, especially if you have the razor-sharp power steering fitted. For a hard-core sportster with few compromises, the driving environment is exceptionally good. Despite being family orientated, Cerberas are even more hard-core and driver focused; the Speed Six is much more usable and has enough performance for the majority over the V8.

BUYING TIPS

Despite TVR's troubled times, spare-parts supply and specialist support is good. Reliability has never been a TVR forte and they need expert attention, especially the AJP engines, which are notoriously fickle and expensive to repair. Due to their nature, TVRs are popular track days cars so look for signs of extreme use – such as a general tired, loose feeling – and more importantly, previous crash damage. However, the real worry is severe chassis rust which really requires the body removed to gauge fully.

PRICES

All represent value for money. Prices start from around £15,000, although it's wiser to budget closer to £20,000 for a sound, solid car with the best busting the £30,000 barrier. Cerberas are priced higher but not by that much, although this may change. The Speed Six is worth less than an equivalent V8 by around £5,000.

VERDICT

These TVRs are the last of the traditional hairy-chested British sports cars and a better prospect than a classic Big Healey (or Morgan) for many. The time to buy is now, as in a decade's time you'll wish you'd bought one for so little!

VOLVO 1800/ES

One of the most recognisable classic cars around, the saintly Volvo 1800 is heaven sent for those wanting a debonair, silver-screen classic that's as easy to buy and own as an MGB.

DATES TO REMEMBER

1961   1800 Coupé launch after debuting at the 1960 Brussels auto show. Based upon the 1.8 Amazon saloon, initial bodies are made by Jensen.

1963   Volvo terminates its contract with Jensen, transferring assembly to Sweden with the car becoming badged as the 1800S (S for Sweden) with 108bhp as opposed to 100bhp.

1968   Biggest change is the adoption of the 1,986cc B20 engine along with dual-circuit braking.

1970   1800E (E being short for Einspritz, German for fuel injection) raises power from 113bhp to 130bhp. Disc brakes now also fitted all round.

1971   ES sports hatch joins Coupé while a three-speed automatic gearbox option arrives.

1972   Coupé dropped; ES surviving only until '73.

DRIVING

From the same era, and with a similar make-up as our MGB GT, it's not surprising that there's a fair few common driving characteristics, such as lusty engines and a soft, roll-prone handling, but for all that the Volvo is an enjoyable classic to drive with Simon Templar-like vigour. For its day, the 1800 was considered quite a fast 2+2. Road tests saw the Volvo hit 60mph in under 10 seconds in fuel-injected form, trucking on to almost 110mph, and overdrive kept the fuel returns reasonable and noise levels down, befitting a car that, as one road test remarked, was 'more a marathon runner than sprinter'.

BUYING TIPS

The MGB analogy extends to easy DIY maintenance and even the Bosch fuel injection is one of the most basic systems (although still expensive to repair). There's good spread of Volvo specialists who can supply routine parts and the two major Volvo owners' clubs are very proactive. Mechanically tough and long lasting, rampant structural rust is the biggest worry, compounded by the fact that many body panels are no longer available, although certain much pricier hand-made ones are. The dashboard top, which if cracked, can't be repaired successfully, and chrome work are pretty pricey with a grille costing £300 alone. Depending on model and year, ATE or

Girling brakes are fitted and, apart from the fact that ATE parts aren't available anymore, there's scant interchangeability opportunities.

PRICES
According to the Volvo Enthusiast's Club, only a third of 400-odd roadworthy cars in the UK are in a saintly condition. The rarest and most desired models are the early 'cow horn bumper' 1800s where no more than fifty remain, resulting in prices as high as £30,000. Otherwise, reckon on £15–£20,000 for nice cars. The Marmite nature of the ES sees regular fluctuation in values, but it can be half the price of an equivalent Coupé.

VERDICT
You can play Simon Templar on a budget, but bear in mind the difficulty and cost of body repairs. The biggest bargains are currently the ES versions but their values are also creeping up so don't delay if you want one.

VOLKSWAGEN BEETLE AND DERIVATIVES

(Historics Auctioneers)

A cult classic, yet there are many strings to a Beetle's bow as owners enjoy a unique driving experience, fantastic backup and a social scene that's second to none. Beetlemania rules!

DATES TO REMEMBER
1949   Transporter and convertible Beetle surface.
1950   Minibus and Kombi join line-up with novel split windscreen (known as Splitties).
1955   Shapely Karmann Ghia coupé and convertible offshoot launched.
1961   Type 3 conventionally styled two-door saloon introduced on stretched floorpan (Variant estate for '63).
1966   1500 (1,493cc) yields 44bhp and standard front disc brakes. Fastback Type 3 added to range with new 1.6-litre power.
1967   Electrics finally become 12V. New look for van line-up, known as 'Bay Window'.

1970   New 1302 'Super Beetle' is added to the range with MacPherson strut front suspension and a 'twin port' 50bhp 1,584cc engine (also for Karmann Ghia).

1973   1303 Beetle identified by a new wraparound windscreen and more modern fascia.

1978   European production ends (world production finally ended in 2003).

1979   T2 (Bay window Transporter) production ends but carries on in Brazil until 2013, using water cooled 1.4-litre power from 2005.

DRIVING

Quirky best describes these rear-engined VWs. Performance from the low-revving engines, even the 1600s, is unhurried but they chug along well once up to speed. Handling needs a watch due to the engine location. It is worst on Beetles prior to 1972, but there's a lot you can do to all to tailor one to your taste. Commercials are blighted by the buffeting at speed and if anything, the squarer-fronted models suffer worse here. The T3 and Type 25, the latter with its improved suspension and weight layout, are the more secure handlers, however. Perhaps the best bit about the Camper experience, though, is its seating position, where you sit high up and well forward, so forward that visibility is excellent.

BUYING TIPS

Running an old-school Volkswagen is simplicity itself. Parts supply is truly excellent thanks to unabating interest in America and there's no shortage of specialists in the UK either, although the cars are easy to work on at home. Not unexpectedly, serious structural rust is the first hurdle and while replacement parts are obtainable, it's not a cheap exercise. Pay special attention to the heat exchangers. As they use engine exhaust fumes for heater warmth, there could be potentially life-threatening consequences if these are rotting through. Steering boxes wear and suffer tight spots, especially on the commercials.

PRICES

Dearest are the Karmann Ghias, Beetle convertibles and T2 Campers, the latter touching £60,000 if truly exceptional, which is as much as three times what Karmann Ghias or Beetle convertibles sell for. The earlier the Beetle saloon, the pricier it is, especially the 'Split' and 'Oval' window models. Cheapest are the 1302/1303s despite being the best drivers – £5,000 will secure a good one.

VERDICT

Excellent starter classics, choose your air-cooled VW well and you'll experience the 'Bug'. Campers are the most trendy, the Karmann Ghias almost a cut-price Porsche 356, while Type 3s are still unfairly overlooked.

VOLKSWAGEN GOLF AND DERIVATIVES

One of the doyens of the Yuppie era, the Golf GTI spawned a whole family feast of great, go-faster, go-getting saloons and coupés. All you have to do is pick the best model for you.

(Author)

DATES TO REMEMBER

1974   Golf Mk1 comes to the UK with a choice of 1,093cc or 1,471cc power, three- and five-door bodies and various trim levels. Sport-hatch Scirocco spin-off has 1.5-litre engine and unique trim levels.

1976   Audi 80 GT-powered Golf GTI is available to special order in left-hand-drive form only.

1979   RHD Golf GTI launched. Scirocco Storm has Golf GTI engine, leather trim and Recaro front sports seats.

1980   Karmann-built Golf GLi convertible joins range.

1981   Five-speed gearbox fitted as standard to GTI, 1,781cc 112bhp engine the following year.

1983   Golf Mk2 evolution launched, but the original convertible continues right up until 1993 until a Mk3 style is adopted.

1986   139bhp 16-valve GTI arrives, sold alongside the 8-valve model.

1989   Corrado coupé replaces Mk2 Scirocco.

1992   Final Mk2 GTIs are registered on a K-plate in the UK. Softer Mk3 goes on sale with uprated 150bhp 16-valve or VR6 2.8 V6 options. 187bhp Corrado replaces G60.

1997   Mk4 Golf rights the wrongs of Mk3 plus now has 1.8-turbo engine option for the GTI or a novel 2.3-litre V5 that delivers the same 150bhp, albeit in a silkier fashion.

DRIVING

Along with the Alfa's super Sud, Golf was the game-changing car of the 1970s. Mk1 Golfs are lean and lively with the GTI still one of the greatest hot hatchbacks ever, even though some Golf gurus claim the Scirocco enjoys slightly sharper handling. The Mk2 Golf took the dynamics a stage further and is regarded as the best all-rounder – less so the Mk2 Scirocco, although this view may be coloured by the car's styling when compared to the original. The Mk3 Golf rather lost the plot but the Mk4 addressed all of this and subsequent Golfs, which includes the riotous all-wheel drive V6 R32, went one better. The Corrado was considered the finest-handling FWD car made and in velvety, vivacious VR6 guise is an affordable sub supercar.

BUYING TIPS

The supply of parts is model dependent with Mk1 Golfs faring the best as they were still produced up until 2009 in South Africa. In contrast, Mk1 Scirocco and Corrado panels can be hard to unearth and all of these VWs rust badly. Be wary over the originality of a late Mk1 GTI Campaign model. These run-out specials featured unique touches and, tellingly, EW letters in the chassis number.

PRICES

Their weight in numbers keeps values low in the main. A sound Mk1 GTI can be yours for around £7,000 but a concours Campaign is more likely to approach £20,000. The Mk2 is still budget-priced and there are plenty of sound examples for £5,000 or less, but the bargain Golf lurks in the Mk3 range. Corrados enjoy a similar price parity to the Mk1 Scirocco, the exception being the VR6, although a good one should still sit under £8,000.

VERDICT

Sporty VWs from the 1980s/90s make great starter classics as well as sensible daily drivers because they are so usable and dependable. The best value lies outside the Golf GTI range, plus some are better cars into the bargain.

ACKNOWLEDGEMENTS

A special big thanks for the images in this book goes to: Historics Auctioneers (www.historics.co.uk) and MagicCarPics (www.magiccarpics.co.uk).

Editorially, my gratitude goes to every car magazine, book and brochure that I have had the pleasure to read and digest.

All images in Part 1 are the author's unless otherwise stated.

ABOUT THE AUTHOR

Alan Anderson is a well-known and respected motoring journalist and self-confessed petrolhead who has written for virtually all the main car magazines since 1983 and edited some ten titles, including *Classic Motoring*.